SOLUTIONS

GUIDEBOOK FOR REBUILDING

AMERICA THE GREAT

LAWRENCE PAUL HEBRON

ISBN: 1461165482

ISBN-13: 9781461165484

Library of Congress Control Number: 2011907625

THIS BOOK IS DEDICATED TO

GOD AND THE UNITED STATES OF AMERICA

WITH SPECIAL APPRECIATION TO

Walter   Ena

Dori

Lisa   Heather

Keith   Ryan

William

and production associates

Wendy A.   Cori F.   Mary N.   Chris P.

TABLE OF CONTENTS

FORWARD

"When you find yourself in a hole, STOP DIGGING!"

Folk wisdom.

"A rut is merely a grave with the ends kicked out."

Folk observation.

America is facing a crisis of nearly unparalleled proportions and severity. There have been few times in our history when we have confronted a danger equal to that of today – and those times all were associated with war: a revolution, a civil war, a world war. It can be argued, in fact, that today's danger is even greater than the crises of yesteryear. Back then the American Spirit was our greatest ally. Today, the American Spirit itself is being destroyed.

It is obvious to any perceptive observer of the current socio-political debate that none of the major contenders in that discussion are offering any solutions that are fundamentally different from the old, hapless, and hopeless policies and programs of the past. We are in a rut (or is it a grave?) and no one is offering us a way to climb out. The major political parties and personalities only disagree about how fast we should keep digging. Precisely when our nation needs a ladder, the politicians only offer us different kinds of shovels. It is time that we the people told them to keep their shovels. We are getting out of here.

This is a guidebook for action – a handbook for doers. It offers unique solutions for the broad, systemic problems of government as well as insights for handling some specific issues such as crime, drugs, illegal immigration, national service, educational reform, and restoring a moral America. It is short. We won't spend much time discussing the nature of problems that we already know we have. Nor will we spend much time considering a crate-load of statistics to define just how bad the problems are. We all know they are bad. We won't cover all the troubles confronting the nation, but we will consider enough of the really bad ones to allow us to effect meaningful and lasting reform. The literary style of this book will be conversational and blunt. There is no intent to impress anyone with a scholarly demeanor. It is said that there is a time for all things under the sun. This is a time for the bold and the decisive. This is a time for warriors, for we are in the fight of our lives – the fight for America's life.

One last thing before we embark. I am no one's lapdog. I will cater to no special interests other than those of God and country. They were good enough for George Washington, and that's good enough for me. As such you can bet that I will be slaughtering a good many sacred cows – but they do make the best hamburgers. I will undoubtedly assail an assumption or two that you hold dear or assault a special interest to which you belong. No apologies. We are all part of the problem, and we all need to make some sacrifices to solve the problem. Remember, it doesn't do much good to have the nicest stateroom on the Titanic if the whole ship goes down. Our ship of state is sinking fast. This is no time for inaction, and it surely is no time to honor the privileged position to which some think they are entitled. We all need to grab a bucket and start bailing. To be sure, we'll get wet and cold. We'll get blisters and sore muscles, and some of us will not make it at all. But if we get this right and get it fast, we can save the ship and all those who remain on board. However, if the ship goes down, there will be no survivors. So, don't think you have a choice in the matter, unless you regard dishonor, dissolution, and death a choice. The time has come for us to unite to re-form a more perfect union. The time has come for us to take pride in the magnitude of our sacrifice, not the magnificence of our privilege. The time has come for Americans to act like Americans.

PART ONE

REFORMING THE GOVERNMENT

CHAPTER ONE

WHEN DREAMS BECOME NIGHTMARES

July 4th, 1776. A dream came true. A nation was born. And a light shone into the darkness. For uncounted generations the children of God had suffered under the yoke of oppressors. Greed and power conspired to subjugate the masses to a force they did not choose and could not resist: the state. The oppressors – the rulers – lived in opulent luxury while their hirelings squeezed the lifeblood from the populace in exchange for a few crumbs from the master's table. Occasionally a new power arose to challenge and even depose the old rulers, but always the fate was the same for the people – they lived, or died, at the whim of the state. The children of the Father suffered grievously. They were persecuted. They were starved. They were imprisoned. They were bought, and they were sold.

The situation seemed hopeless. But the oppressors had forgotten something, if they had ever understood it at all. The Father, you see, had given his children a piece of Himself – a piece that could not forever tolerate oppression. Deep within each child, an ember still glowed. A Voice called out, "For freedom I have set you free." The Voice was heard, and the children cried out, ***"Give me liberty or give me death!"*** The children took up the cause, and they took up arms. They fought. They died. They suffered. They sacrificed. But they would not give up, and finally they prevailed. Their reward? A government of the people, by the people, and for the people. Finally, finally, they would live their lives as they saw fit, and they would let others do the same, without state masters to dictate their destiny. They would make their own. Sometimes they would succeed. Sometimes they would fail. But it was their life to live. And the children gave praise to the Father for this one nation under God.

We grew. We prospered. We prevailed. And then we began to forget. The Deceivers and charlatans saw a chance. They pointed to flaws and failings and promised that they could do better – if only the children would surrender control of their lives to them – if only the state could be made more powerful in order to save the children from themselves. That liberty, which had been purchased at such a dear price, was now to be traded away for the promise of security. And what about that God Who had so faithfully provided that liberty to His children? Well, we were told that we must no longer mention His name in public affairs. To do so would be old-fashioned and abusive; and, besides, He was really no longer relevant to the affairs of state. We had other gods now. Gods that would lead us to a perfect, progressive society.

Sadly, the children listened to the Deceivers. They made the terrible trade. They exchanged their liberty for the promise of security, and they achieved – neither. History could have told us what to expect. The problem with History, however, is that it teaches tough lessons – lessons that a comfortable people would rather ignore. This is why empires ultimately fall. Their initial strengths lead to power which leads to wealth which leads to comfort which leads to sloth which leads to decline and defeat and dissolution. Similarly, America's initial strengths have led to power and wealth and comfort. Many Americans have grown complacent, soft, and pudgy; they assume that America's everlasting greatness is a foregone conclusion – no matter how ignobly and irresponsibly we behave. Many Americans have come to believe that we can ignore – even violate – the lessons of History with impunity. We cannot, but there is always an abundance of unscrupulous Deceivers eager to tell the people what they want to hear instead of what they need to hear. They sing the Siren's song and tempt the people into foolish beliefs and destructive behaviors. They know that you can convince most people to jump into a pile of manure as long as you cover it over with enough rose petals. Ultimately the people will pay the price, but the Deceivers don't care. They achieve the power, prestige, prominence, and prosperity that are their true goals.

We the people are now paying the price for having listened to the Deceivers and the charlatans. Lives have been cheapened and wasted by drugs, addiction, promiscuous relationships, and selfish obsessions. Families have been shattered by adultery, divorce, and abortion. Communities have been ravaged by the onslaught of a growing criminal population and the inability to contain it. The once robust economy has buckled and bowed beneath the weight of excessive taxation and an increasingly unproductive populace. And the once proud nation – that shining city on the hill – has sunk deeper and deeper into the pit of debt and disrepute and despair and darkness. The dream of 1776 has become the nightmare of today. The old master – the state – has returned. But what can we do? What can we do?

What can we do? Remember the ember. It is not dead – it cannot die. It still smolders deep within the breast of each of the Father's children – deep within each one of us. Fan it, and let our enemies fear it. We, by God, are Americans. Two hundred and thirty years ago we rocked the world. By God, it's time to do it again.

Before we proceed, however, we must be clear about two things. First, we will not save our nation by doing more of the same things that got us into this mess in the first place. Ultimately, none of the major political parties today is offering anything substantially different from the bad medicine that made us sick to begin with. Our choices seem to be between Tweedledee, Tweedledum, and Tweedledumber. Virtually all our political pundits today are not only using the same cookbook, they are working from the same recipe. Some just add a little less salt, a few more carrots, but always plenty of pork. Talking about "change" has been popular for some time now; but in fact, no one is changing the channel – they just fiddle with the volume. More of the same *will not work*.

Second, there will be pain. A great athlete who lets himself go – who becomes weak and obese – cannot achieve the fitness he once enjoyed without suffering and sacrifice. That is not a pleasant choice, but it beats the alternative: disease, disrepute, and death. We Americans have let ourselves go for too long to expect an easy, painless recovery. Shame on the politicians who lied to us, but even more shame on us for listening. We should have known better and sent the charlatans packing before they ever had the chance to foul this great nation. We should have, but we didn't; and now we must pay a heavy price or die a shameful death.

In the chapters that follow some new ways will be offered for solving some old problems. They will not be easy nor will they be pleasant. They will be vehemently opposed by the old guard that prospers from the present adversity of America: the cup-bearers, hirelings, and sycophants of the secular, progressive state. In fact, I strongly suspect that *every* reader will find some bitter pills in this prescription that is being offered. Good. That attests to a certain evenhandedness. Nothing less, however, will work. As the daunting prospect of war with Great Britain loomed before the revolutionaries, Benjamin Franklin warned that we must all hang together or we will surely all hang separately. Today, we face the reality that we all must sacrifice as individuals or we will surely all be sacrificed as a nation. I will spare no one's sacred cows for reasons of political expediency nor correctness. I will not tell you what you want to hear; I will tell you what I believe you need to hear, and I expect you to muster the courage to do what needs to be done. Anything less is un-American; and if ever there were a time for us to act like Americans, this is it.

CHAPTER TWO

PREMISES

Most people do not **construct** political philosophies and programs for action. They **gather** them – much like a child collects gaily-colored balloons. "This red one looks nice. I'll take it. Ooh, there's a pretty blue one. Grab it. And see that lovely green one over there? I want it, too." And so on until a beautiful balloon bouquet has been assembled. It may look nice, but there is no mutual support, no interconnectedness, nothing that holds it all together to provide synergy and strength to either the child or the bouquet. The first stormy wind or sudden shock that causes the child to loosen her grip and – there they go! The yellow one cannot keep the pink one from floating away. The purple one can do nothing to keep the orange one from popping when it blows into a tree branch. So it is with most people's views on politics and on solutions for political problems. They **collect** nice-sounding slogans. "'Ecologically friendly', that seems responsible. 'Pro-choice', my, that sounds gracious and tolerant. 'Gay rights', wow, what a happy concept. 'Change', yep, that's what we need!" And so on until a lovely political bouquet has been compiled. Unfortunately, there usually is very little more than the most superficial consideration given to the merits of the various ideas or whether all the ideas combined are mutually supporting or even compatible. Such a jumble of ill-founded and inconsistent notions will inevitably lead to foolish policies, disastrous practices, and ineffective remedies. Such a jumble of ill-founded and inconsistent notions have led us to our current predicament, and they most certainly will not lead us out of it.

Our current problems are so great, and the impending disaster is so imminent, that we cannot afford to waste any time or other resources floundering about looking for solutions. We need to hit upon the right approach right away. To accomplish this we must begin with sound premises. A "premise", as the word is used here, refers to a basic belief or principle which serves as a foundation or source or guide for subsequent reasoning and the development of policies and practices. Sound – or true – premises are essential to the development of successful policies and practices. If one's beginning is flawed, it is pretty hard to achieve a good ending; and as I said, we simply have no time to waste on false starts or reckless experimentation. We need to be on target right out of the barrel. So, how do we do this? Easy. We go with what we know works.

Over two centuries ago our Founders hit upon a providential mix of premises that resulted in the greatest nation in the history of mankind. (I make no apologies for this apparent jingoism. If you can prove me wrong, go for it.) Oh, they didn't get it all right – slavery is bad and women should be allowed to vote – but they got most of it right. The result was the creation of a society that stunned History and inspired much of the world – and with good reasons. Their success was so phenomenal, so unique, and so unrivaled that I cannot think of a better way to heal our nation than to follow the example of those who founded it.

Now, there is no place in this brief book for a detailed review of the writings and philosophies of men such as John Locke, William Blackstone, and Charles Montesquieu who inspired the Patriot Founders. This is a handbook for action. All I will do here is state three fundamental and mutually supporting premises which guided the Founders and which **must** guide us.

First: We must respect and protect the enjoyment of individual liberties to the greatest degree consistent with the operation of a civil society. Briefly, a "civil society" is defined as a community where people have the opportunity to pursue their legitimate objectives in relative peace. I must emphasize in the strongest terms that our obligation is to provide individuals with the **opportunity** to pursue their ambitions. We cannot and must not seek to **guarantee** the achievement of those ambitions; but we must guarantee the opportunity to peacefully pursue them. There is no collective, utopian objective (such as a job for all, healthcare for all, a pension for all, etc.) which supercedes the importance of maximizing and protecting individual liberties. In point of fact, the best way to pursue even these whimsical, utopian notions is by enriching a person's liberties, not by extinguishing them. Ultimately, the only ones who truly benefit from the pursuit of such utopian objectives through the use of state agencies are the ones who administer these state agencies as well as their lackeys and co-conspirators. All others are robbed of their liberties and their earnings.

Second: We must restrict the size of government at all levels to the absolute minimum necessary to maintain a civil society. This goal is inescapably connected with the first goal of preserving and maximizing individual liberties. It *must* be understood that big government and big liberty are absolutely incompatible. In other words, liberties shrink as government grows. Governments function through the making, administering, and adjudicating of laws; but laws, by their very nature, usually work to limit liberties. Think about it. We do not need laws to require people to do what they are going to do naturally. As essential as breathing is to life, I am unaware of any law anywhere on Earth that establishes standards for breathing (like minimum, average, and maximum number of breaths per minute; average cubic liters of air inhaled per minute; etc.). People are going to breathe. On the other hand, we do not need laws to keep people from doing something that no one in his right mind is going to do – such as bathing in sulfuric acid. We only need laws to make people do something that they would not otherwise do (like pay income taxes) or to keep them from doing something that they would otherwise do (like driving too fast to be safe). Now, some amount of laws is necessary to maintain the "civil" society we mentioned earlier; but it must be understood that almost any law will work to limit individual liberties. Hence, the bigger the government the smaller the liberties; and this works against the first objective mentioned above.

Third: We must work to re-create and preserve a moral society. This is an issue that has been given little more than cursory lip-service in recent political discussions, and yet it is ***absolutely indispensable*** to the accomplishment of meaningful political reform. The proponents of big government and little liberty don't have a clue about how to repair this nation. Unfortunately, the proponents of little government and big liberty are also barking up the wrong tree if they do not first insist upon a ***moral society***.

The Tree of Liberty cannot grow in any kind of soil. It is fairly selective; and if we expect liberty to flourish, we must provide the fertile ground in which it can take root, survive, and thrive. A moral populace is the necessary pre-condition without which "more freedom" and "less government" are suicidal objectives. Rebuilding a moral society is absolutely essential to rebuilding a prosperous and free America; and yet this is something that none of the major political parties is talking about in any serious way. Until they do, we should not take them seriously. We'll have more to say about this in Chapter Eleven.

So, in a nutshell, what do we need to do? We need to rebuild the United States of America spiritually, politically, and economically according to Biblical principles and the ideals of the Founders. This does not mean that we have to do everything the way the Founders did. Many circumstances have changed, and it would be foolish to address these modern circumstances with antiquated tools. However, whereas circumstances may have changed, basic realities about human nature have not. Since the Founders did such a brilliant job of understanding and dealing with these realities – and especially since we have not – we would be well-advised to once again follow their lead.

Now, let's get to the particulars.

CHAPTER THREE

GOVERNMENT IS THE PROBLEM

Does it make any sense to trust the problem-causer to be the problem-solver? Of course not. If the problem-causer knew how to avoid the problem in the first place, then why didn't he? He must have had some vested interest in the course of events which led to the problem; which means he cannot be trusted with handling the interests of others because he is willing to betray those interests in order to enrich his own. Surely, this is one of the definitions of "evil." (Think about everything that is called a "sin" in the Bible – it always boils down to someone selfishly pursuing his own interests to the detriment of another.) On the other hand, if the problem-causer did not anticipate the unfolding of events that would lead to the problem, then he is incompetent and should not be trusted with managing the interests of others. Evil or incompetent – these are pretty much the only ways to describe "problem-causers."

Now, look around – survey the disaster, both present and impending. A strong argument can be made that the federal government of the United States – or more accurately, those who have managed the affairs of the federal government over the last several decades – is the greatest problem-causer in the history of mankind. So, are those who have managed these affairs evil or incompetent? Well, if these managers (legislators, executives, and jurists) truly believed that their policies would work, then they are incompetent. Still, I find it hard – not impossible – but hard to believe that there are that many stupid people in government. This leads us to the sad conclusion that there must be a great many evil people in government. How does this evil manifest itself? Again sadly, in a variety of ways, but here is a very common method used by the proponents of big government (which, sadly again, includes both "liberals" and "conservatives" because exceedingly few of either type have consistently fought against all "pork-barrel" spending and earmarks). Politicians make promises of "benefits" to a particular constituency in order to get them to vote for that politician. These "benefits" rarely enrich the general populace, but the general populace is required to pay for them through their tax dollars. Therefore, as the federal budget swells, so too does the burden of the taxpayer and the size of the national deficit – which, in turn, will cause even greater problems for the citizenry in the future. So, the politician uses our money to buy votes and in the process undermines the well-being of both the nation and the individual. He knows what he is doing is harmful, but he does it anyway in order to secure and perpetuate power for himself. Evil. Here is another example of evil manifesting itself in government, this time by a government employee and not by an elected official. An honorable woman whom I know used to work for a government agency that oversaw the administration of welfare payments. She told me of a "field trip" which she took to check on the validity of a claim made by a young woman who was receiving several hundred dollars a month of taxpayer funded welfare money. This young woman was not needy. In fact it became quickly apparent that the taxpayer's donation was merely providing the young woman with some extra spending money, some of which went to her parents for "rent." Both the young woman and her parents were stunned when they realized that someone would actually check up on them. Overwhelmed by shame for their fraudulent claim (and probably more than a little afraid of retribution) they asked to be removed from the welfare rolls. The conscientious public official returned to her office with a warm and fuzzy feeling that she had protected the public interest and saved the taxpayers some money. Her boss didn't feel the same way. Essentially, she was reprimanded, and the following day her supervisor contacted the young cheat and her parents and talked them into going back onto the welfare rolls. Why? The more people on welfare in the supervisor's region meant a bigger budget, a bigger staff, and a bigger salary for him. Serving the public interest was not the true objective of the supervisor. Job security and empire-building were his motives, and the taxpayer gets to foot the bill. Evil – and commonplace.

Suppose you hired a painter to paint your house, and he did a terrible job. He used the wrong color and dribbled paint everywhere inside and out. The paint that actually made it to the walls was streaked and caked. He broke your windows, trampled your plants, scared your pets, and was mean to your kids. And if all that weren't bad enough, he took five times as long to finish the job as he had promised and then asked for more money than had been agreed to. Would you hire him again or recommend him to others? Of course not. If you went to a dentist who pulled the wrong tooth and nicked a nerve causing the left side of your face to permanently droop and the right side to coil up in a ghoulish grin all while you had to endure excruciating pain, would you hire him again? Of course not. If you went to a restaurant that served you a foul-tasting meal (not fowl-tasting – that would be okay if you ordered chicken or turkey) complete with dog hairs in the potatoes and insects in your beverage, would you go back? Of course not. Well, government has been consistently failing us and selling out our children's future for several decades now. Why do we keep turning to them to solve so many of our problems? There are other options.

People have been arguing about whether the government should do more or less for a long time. Generally speaking, the "do more" people have been winning. The political debate gets pretty twisted and confusing at times, and this confusion has worked to obscure a basic reality that should settle the argument once and for all. So, let's cut to the chase and finish this now. Name five things that the federal government does well. "Well" is defined as effectively and efficiently. "Effectively" means that the goal is accomplished. "Efficiently" means that the goal is accomplished with a minimum of waste and expense. Okay, five things – name them. Having a little trouble? How about three? The federal government does thousands of things. Can't you think of even three that are done well? Two? One??? The most common – and often the only – answer I get to this question is "the military." I agree that our troops are the greatest; but then I remind the listener that I **did** say "efficiently", and there is no way that the Department of Defense wins any awards for efficiency, and everyone knows it. At this point the listener's eyes again roll upward apparently seeking an answer on the ceiling, and I hear a prolonged and profound silence. Well, if you cannot even think of five – or three or one – things that the federal government does well, then why do we keep turning to them to solve all our problems? It's pretty much as Ronald Reagan observed, government isn't the answer to our problems. Government is the problem. And not only is this true, it pretty much has been true throughout the entire history of government. Our Founders understood this, which is why they worked so hard to limit the scope and power of the state. So I ask again, why do we keep turning to history's greatest problem-causer to solve so many of our problems?

In the last chapter we declared that our second premise is to restrict the size of government at all levels to the absolute minimum necessary to maintain a civil society. As we noted back then, part of the reason for this is that liberty shrinks as government grows. Another basic reason is that the government simply does not do very many things very well, nor should it be expected to do so. Government is a social "tool" – a device for accomplishing something – just like a hammer is a device for pounding nails. Like other tools it is well-designed to do a very few things well. There is a whole universe of other things, however, that it does not do well. A spoon, for example, is well-designed to deliver soup and other delicacies from your bowl to your mouth. It would be a poor choice, however, if you needed to dig a hole or chop down a tree. Similarly, the government is reasonably well-suited to do a very few things. Expecting it to do more than this is foolish; and yet the advocates of big government keep seeking more and more things for it to do. This is a natural and inevitable tendency; and since it is a tendency that inevitably leads to the suffering and oppression of the general populace, it **must** be vigorously and consistently opposed.

The Founders understood this. In fact, they were so fearful of a large and powerful government that their first attempt at forming a union failed. The national government created by the Articles of Confederation (our first constitution) was too weak to get the job done. When the Founders met in 1787 and ended up writing a new Constitution, their intent was not to create a big and powerful national government, but rather a national government that was a *little* bit bigger and a *little* bit more powerful – but just a little. They still feared a burly national government and tried to prevent it with a variety of restrictions which they wrote into the Constitution. They actually did a pretty good job, but they may have underestimated the creativity and unscrupulousness of future politicians and justices who had no qualms about redefining the Constitution in ways that grotesquely betrayed the original intent.

Now that we have established our premises and demonstrated the folly of expecting the great problem-causer to miraculously become the Messiah-like problem-solver, let's look at some specific ways to shrink the federal government and keep it shrunk.

CHAPTER FOUR

ENTITLE THIS

Okay, this is where that pain I wrote about in the first chapter will start to kick in. It will be impossible to accomplish any kind of meaningful and substantial reform of the federal government without taking a chain saw to the various "entitlement programs" administered by the federal government. Entitlement expenditures have become the largest sector of the federal budget. Entitlement programs have become the chief tool that the Deceivers and political charlatans use to control our behavior and limit our liberties. It simply will be impossible to eradicate the debt (which is crushing us and destroying our children's future) and restore individual freedoms without eliminating these entitlement programs. That's right, *eliminate*, not just cut back – *eliminate!*

"Entitlement programs" are those activities of government which provide various resources – though usually monetary ones – to individuals and groups which are deemed to be "entitled" to them because they meet some qualifying standard. For example, if you do not make a certain amount of money, you are "entitled" to welfare. If you are sick or injured and cannot pay for your own medical expenses, you are "entitled" to government-funded healthcare. If you are old enough, you are "entitled" to government pension payments (that is, Social Security).

Helping the "needy" is certainly a worthwhile objective. I strongly commend those who do it and urge others to follow their example. "Urging", however, is all that I am morally entitled to do. It is a violation of our first and second premises to force individuals to help some "entitled" group by compelling those individuals to surrender their earnings and liberties (through taxation) in order to pay for the massive government bureaucracies which administer these programs (thereby increasing the size of government and entrusting more areas of our lives to their evil or incompetent management). So what about the third premise of establishing and preserving a moral society? Shouldn't we be helping the needy? Of course, so long as the help is voluntary. Unfortunately, many of our social activists seem to overlook the fact that compulsion is not compassion – it is coercion, which is immoral. We simply are not justified in forcing people to help the less fortunate. Jesus never grabbed anyone's arm, twisted it behind his back, and wrenched it upward until the victim cried out, "Messiah!" He told people what they should do and then gave them the free choice to exercise their free will. We should follow His example.

Virtually all entitlement programs, subsidies, and bailouts (which usually work out to be the same thing under different names) should be eliminated. I use the qualifier, "virtually", only because there is a very small list of agencies and activities which technically fall under the category of being an "entitlement" program and yet which are morally and contractually appropriate. (An example would be the network of veteran's hospitals which provide medical services to those injured in the course of performing their duties for their country.) Now, in case you were wondering, yes, this hit list includes all welfare programs, unemployment compensation, subsidies to "troubled" industries, Medicare, Medicaid, and – brace yourself – Social Security.

Undoubtedly, scores of questions and objections immediately arise upon making such a bold statement. I will deal with a few of the most important of these here. Some other issues will be addressed in future chapters. Keep in mind, however, that all the recommendations in this handbook are intended to make things better, not worse. Many readers right now are undoubtedly outraged and wondering (probably at the top of their lungs and with clenched fists), "How can eliminating Social Security, Medicare, Medicaid, unemployment compensation, welfare, and subsidies to troubled industries possibly make things better!?!" This is because you have completely bought into the idea that the government is your friend and that it is the best and maybe the only way to solve our problems. This is not true, but as long as you believe it to be true you will keep looking to the problem-causer to be your problem-solver – and we've all seen how poorly that has worked out. So, let us take a look at why these beliefs, policies, and practices are hurting, not helping us; and why we will never be able to set sail on a new course until we cut the chains on these anchors which are not only holding us back but dragging us down.

I will use the example of the almightiest of sacred cows – Social Security – to illustrate some of the problems inherent with these entitlement programs and why we must rid ourselves of them. Back during the Great Depression (which, by the way, a study by Nobel Prize winning economist Milton Freedman proved rather conclusively was brought about by ill-advised monetary policies of the Federal Reserve System and not by a failure of the capitalist system) Franklin D. Roosevelt proposed and established Social Security. Although its responsibilities have been expanded over the years, its main purpose has been to create a "safety net" pension for the elderly. Is this a nice idea? Yes. Is this a good way to accomplish it? No. Let's see why.

Keep in mind that neither the Social Security Act nor the Social Security Administration has done anything to create "extra wealth" which can be used to assist the elderly. They simply redistribute the wealth that already exists, taking it from those who have it and giving it to those who do not. In fact, it can be argued that Social Security reduces the supply of wealth because it punishes (through taxation) people for being productive, thereby weakening the incentive to be productive. Now, why is there a need to redistribute this wealth and provide these pensions? There seem to be two main reasons. First, some people who were in a position to provide for their own pensions did not. Second, some people simply did not earn enough to be able to provide for their own pensions. If you are in the first category, shame on you; now suffer the consequences of your irresponsibility because we are not going to let you steal from those who were more responsible than you and who made personal sacrifices throughout their lives while you "partied hearty." (Is anyone recalling images of ants and grasshoppers right about now?) If you are in the second category, why were you unable – or is it "unwilling" – to earn more? Is it because you didn't apply yourself at school; you were lazy or dishonest on the job; you destroyed your productive talents with drugs or alcohol; you wasted your money on "toys" and fun instead of planning for the future; or you made foolish decisions about selecting a vocation? Again, shame on you; now suffer the consequences of your irresponsibility because we are not going to let you steal from those who were more responsible than you and who worked harder and smarter than you did. Ah, but what about that relatively small category of people who truly were unable to be more productive and prosperous through no fault of their own? You may ask, "How are we going to take care of them?" My answer: "That's why we have families, churches, and charities; all of which tend to do a much more conscientious job of caring for the needs of the less fortunate than an impersonal, inefficient, and corrupt federal bureaucracy. What's more, all of these families, churches, and charities would have hundreds of billions of extra dollars to spend on such humanitarianism if the federal government weren't soaking up all that money like some kind of malignant sponge."

Our first objection to Social Security and other entitlement programs is that they force an unconscionable transfer of wealth from those who worked hard to earn it to those who did not. It denies individuals the opportunity to make personal decisions about their own property while it undermines the responsibility to do so. All of this is extremely corrosive to both individual and collective interests. If people are denied the opportunity to make decisions about their own property, there isn't much incentive to work hard in order to acquire that property. Productivity decreases and the net worth of the nation drops – which reduces our ability to help anyone. If individual responsibility is weakened, then "collective responsibility" is required to fill the gap; and this invariably results in the accumulation of dangerous levels of power in the hands of a few "administrators." This is why we revolted in the first place and why we have continued the righteous fight for freedom throughout the centuries. Ask George the Third, Hitler, and Stalin.

Another important point to remember about the redistribution of wealth is that there are only two relevant variables which describe the nature of this transfer:

whether the transfer is voluntary or involuntary and whether the transfer is direct or indirect. Let's see how this works out. Under a "voluntary-direct" exchange, the donor, of his own free will, gives directly to the recipient. Example: giving to a beggar. In a "voluntary-indirect" transfer the donor, again of his own free will, gives to some organization which then passes the contribution on to the recipient. Example: giving to a church or charity. In the case of an "involuntary-direct" exchange, the donor is coerced against his will to make a contribution directly to the recipient. Example: a hold-up or mugging. Under the "involuntary-indirect" method, the donor is coerced against his will to make a contribution to some organization which then passes that contribution on to the recipient. Examples: gang "protection" levies and federal entitlement programs. We see from this model that the federal government has put itself in league with robbers, thieves, carjackers, gangsters, and muggers.

Our next objection to Social Security (and many other entitlement programs) is that the program itself is fatally flawed and destined to fail. Despite all the years you may have faithfully made your Social Security contributions, there is no pot of gold with your name on it sitting somewhere waiting until you hit some magic age – which seems to be subject to change. There is a formula for determining what your monthly income will be, but there are no funds patiently awaiting your retirement. Social Security is neither an investment nor an annuity in the true and legitimate sense of these words. Franklin

Roosevelt and his buddies succeeded in creating a Ponzi scheme of such dimensions that it makes Bernie Madoff look like a piker. Let's be clear: if any of us attempted what the federal government has done, we would be hunted down, arrested, indicted, tried, convicted, and sentenced to a very long jail term. So, why isn't the federal government being charged? Well, remember what we said before: it is the job of the government to make, administer, and adjudicate laws. When you're holding all the cards, you can bet the game will go your way. Under the current system the government holds the cards; we the people do not.

Ponzi schemes are illegal because they are destined to fail and to cheat a great many people – and so are Social Security and other entitlement programs. The name of this particular con job comes from Charles Ponzi who was an Italian swindler. Here's how it works. A group of people are convinced to "invest" in some kind of plan that appears legitimate. The manager of the scheme, however, does not invest the money. He keeps most of it but returns a substantial amount to his investors in a short period of time making it look as though the plan is working extremely well. The "investors" may receive a ten, fifteen, or twenty percent return on investment in just a few months. The first tier of investors is natu-rally encouraged to contribute more money while telling friends and relatives about this golden opportunity. This creates a second, larger tier of investors who are similarly rewarded in a short period of time. This, in turn, leads to a third and fourth tier and so on. (A graphic chart of these tiers of investors would fan out from the top down creating a pyramid shape which inspired the synonym for Ponzi schemes: the Pyramid scheme.) Little, if any, of the money being contributed is actually invested into anything that will generate true growth of the investors' money. Much of the money goes to the crooked manager. Now, it is often the case that the people at the top of the pyramid also can do very well. However, the "investment opportunity" ultimately fails for most of the investors because there simply was no real growth of money, and much of the money that was contributed was siphoned off by the manager/crook and given to early investors to "salt the mine." The same fate is inevitable for Social Security. Much of the money you put into FICA every payday goes out the door very shortly thereafter to pay for current demands – that is, it is paid to those higher in the pyramid than you are. In point of fact Social Security is already dead; cowardly politicians just keep pouring perfume on the corpse to fool the rest of us and to keep them from having to deal with a very harsh reality. If we don't terminate Social Security soon, Social Security will soon terminate us.

Government-coerced, taxpayer funded entitlement programs constitute an immoral and unjustifiable con-fiscation of people's property while at the same time denying the people the opportunity and responsibility to take care of their own interests as they see fit – you know, all that "life, liberty and pursuit of happiness" stuff.

Furthermore, they invariably contain a poison pill which insures their failure. Social Security is an unsustainable Ponzi scheme. Welfare programs become self-perpetuating because they weaken families and destroy a sense of individual responsibility – both of which are critical for getting people off of welfare. Unemployment compensation discourages productivity which is the source of jobs.

Oh, but the list goes on. Even if this forced redistribution of wealth were not immoral, and even if these programs did not contain a suicidal poison pill, there are other reasons for discontinuing them. One of the biggest is the inefficiency, waste, fraud, and graft that is rampant within the government. The government simply is not a very good choice for accomplishing many of the objectives which have been entrusted to it. In fact, it is a downright horrible choice in many instances. The ironic thing is that most of us know this, and yet we still ask, "What is the **government** going to do?" whenever a problem arises. This demonstrates how well we have been brainwashed by those who have a vested interest in big government.

Well, if government operations are so ineffective and inefficient – remember how much trouble you had thinking of five things the federal government does well? – why do we keep looking to them for salvation? It seems to be due largely to an unholy alliance between malevolence and ignorance. Many of the people who advocate government activism know full well that it won't work – or, more correctly, that it will not solve the problem for which the government action is urged. On the other hand, government activism works very well to gather and consolidate power where these politicians can get their hands on it – and this, for many, is the true objective. Power is taken from the people and given to the persons: the persons in control of the trillions of dollars which used to belong to the people, and the persons who control the government agencies which distribute those trillions of dollars. Remember: whoever controls the purse strings also controls the nose rings – you know, the devices used by ranchers to lead cattle about, like to the slaughter. Of course, no one in his right mind – and especially not independent-minded Americans – would ever knowingly allow anyone to insert such a nose ring and attach the leash by which we can be led around. So how do the Deceivers and charlatans entice us to buy into these government programs? They start off by pointing to imperfections in the society (poor people who are hungry, old people who have no pension, sick people who have no health insurance, etc.). This isn't difficult since we will never achieve perfection this side of Heaven. They then spin a heart-rending tale of woe and ask how any compassionate person could possibly refuse to help. Next, they propose to offer that help through the government, which is big and strong and looks like a worthy candidate to be a protector. Anyone who opposes these plans is painted as a heartless, greedy monster. Most of the people who propose such schemes are smart enough to know that they won't work; but if the scheme can be implemented, it will work to give the Deceivers and charlatans more power, which is their real objective. They then play on the ignorance of the masses in matters of economics and government to fool many people into supporting these programs. Once the programs are implemented the Deceivers and charlatans continue their smoke and mirrors campaign by putting the spotlight on a few engaging success stories to fool the masses into believing the plan is working and should be continued (and there always will be some successes – even Ponzi schemes enrich a few investors).

Sadly, this deception often works – at least for a while, until the inherent problems of the system create difficulties so great that they can no longer be ignored – like now. By that time, however, the Deceivers and charlatans have not only developed a huge vested interest in continuing the programs, they also have acquired the power that enables them to do so. And a great deal of this power is rooted in the support of the various constituencies who also have now developed a vested interest in the benefits distributed by the Deceivers and charlatans. It kind of reminds you of the tactics used by drug dealers; doesn't it? Once you get the "clients" hooked on the product (insert the nose ring), you can lead them about with little resistance because they are so afraid of losing the product – even when the clients know that the product is killing them. In fact, let's be even more blunt. Example 1: the drug dealer lures the prospective client into using drugs by alluding to its many alleged benefits and by offering a low price. The client buys the pitch and becomes addicted. The client finds out all the downside of drug use, but it is too late. He feels he needs both the product and the pusher who controls the product. The drug dealer now has tremendous power. The price of the product soars while the health of the client is destroyed, but the addiction continues and the pusher prospers. Example 2: the charlatan politician lures the prospective client (voters) to support Social Security by claiming many benefits and promising a low cost. The voter buys the pitch and becomes addicted. The client finds out all the downside of Social Security, but it is too late. He feels he needs both the product and the politicians who control it. The politicians now have tremendous power. The price of the product soars while the national economic health is destroyed, but the addiction continues and the politician prospers.

We the people must come to understand that a great deal of what the big-government politicians are offering us is for their benefit, not ours. Why, for example, do you think they take money from the local communities and then offer it back to these communities – but only *if* the community members agree to spend the money *on* the things the politicians want to support and *in the way* the politicians want to support them? It's all about building and protecting the interests of the Deceivers and charlatan politicians. Example: "We'll give you money to upgrade your roads or schools or libraries *so long as you* pay 'prevailing wages' and hire a given percentage of people from a certain race or who are disabled." Translation: we are going to use your money to buy the votes of union members, members of that racial group, and the disabled. Or, "We'll give you money to build 'green technologies' or a high speed railroad system to benefit your community." Translation: we are going to use your money to buy the votes of people in certain industries and especially the managers and investors in those industries. If the national politicians truly had the interests of the local community at heart, they would simply leave the money in these communities so the local citizenry could spend it as they saw fit.

Another excellent example of how the Deceivers and charlatans manipulate the flow of money to benefit themselves – not us – can be seen in the "stimulus" programs that the federal government orchestrated in order to respond to the harmful effects of the Great Recession in the early twenty-first century. Several hundreds of billions of dollars (our money) were poured into the economy to "stimulate" it. This resulted in a huge addition to the federal deficit. Well, we might ask, if the government is willing to incur a debt anyway, why not just cut our taxes by an amount equal to the stimulus package? Wouldn't this have the same effect as taking our money out of the economy and then putting it back in? Well, yes and **NO**. Cutting taxes would provide more money for consumers and taxpayers to spend or save – which presumably would stimulate the economy – but it would deny the Deceivers and charlatans control over where that money went. The crooked politicians didn't just want to stimulate the economy. They used the crisis to gain control of hundreds of billions of dollars which they then spent to secure and perpetuate their own power.

As we have seen the growth of the "entitlement sector" of the federal government is as destructive to our national well-being as the growth of a malignant tumor is to the well-being of an individual. Let us briefly summarize the main points of this chapter.

1. It is morally insufferable to extort this kind of transfer of wealth. By what twisted line of reasoning can we possibly justify taking money which rightfully belongs to the person who earned it in order to pursue "social goals" which either do not benefit that individual or which rightly should be that individual's responsibility to accomplish?

2. These programs undermine and weaken individual responsibility. This, in turn, stifles the productivity which supports the general welfare. It also leads to "collective responsibility" which takes power away from the individual and concentrates it in the hands of the "administrators."

3. These entitlement programs invariably contain a fatal flaw which insures their failure and jeopardizes the well-being of the nation.

4. Both history and common sense demonstrate that the government is a spectacularly foolish choice for accomplishing many community and

personal objectives. Government agencies have consistently proven themselves to be inefficient, wasteful, and subject to graft and corruption. The private sector is a much wiser choice for accomplishing most of these goals.

5. Whereas there are some individuals who truly believe that these entitlement programs are justifiable, both history and common sense have conclusively proven these people to be wrong. Given the manifold manifestations of the failures of these programs, those who continue to support them must be either inordinately ignorant (unaware of these failures) or profoundly malevolent (aware of the failures but willing to accept the destruction of the national well-being in order to enhance their own personal well-being). The time has long since passed for us to end our dependence upon the incompetent and the evil.

The only prudent course of action is a radical "entitlectomy": we cut it out. In so doing we reduce the federal budget by far more than half. We can also eliminate many of the departments of the federal government which exist to administer these programs. The government becomes smaller, less expensive, and more manageable. The people become stronger, freer, and richer. So, how do we do this and how do we prevent the malignancy from returning? That will be the subject of the next chapter.

CHAPTER FIVE

A POUND OF CURE; AN OUNCE OF PREVENTION

It was argued in the preceding chapter that we must eliminate virtually all of the federal entitlement programs and the agencies of government which administer them. How do we do this? I agree that it is usually better to quickly yank off a bandage than to slowly peel it back. However, I am not sure that this is the proper analogy in this situation. Much to our shame we have allowed the Deceivers to create these programs, take our money to fund them, and cause us to become dependent upon them. Still, we **have** become dependent upon them, much like a junkie is dependent upon the drug dealer and his poison. Now our task is to free ourselves from this addiction while doing as little additional damage as possible. True, it would be just for us to go "cold turkey" and suffer the full consequences of our folly, but mercy is also a worthy objective; and if

Americans can muster the determination and courage to do what is necessary to end this dependency, I would certainly like to see it done in as gentle a manner as is practicable. Accordingly, I would recommend that we phase out Social Security and Medicare over a period of perhaps fifteen years. This would allow our current generation of retirees to make a gradual transition from their dependence upon the support they were hoodwinked into anticipating and counting upon. It would also allow time for the next generation of retirees to prepare for self-sufficiency. I would recommend that we phase out all the other entitlement programs over a much shorter period of time – perhaps three years. This also would give time for individuals and private organizations to prepare for self-sufficiency. All the government agencies involved with the dispensation of entitlement funds would similarly be phased out over the same three years. This would give time for the employees of these agencies to find productive occupations, and there ought to be a substantial number of these considering all the hundreds of billions of dollars that will be returned to the private sector.

Reducing the size and scope of the federal government is only part of the formula for our recovery. We also must build into this process an ironclad mechanism for preventing this from ever happening again. There always will be tyrannical idealists who believe that every problem can be solved if only we have the right medicine and if only we can force everybody to swallow it. There always will be the ignorant who know so little about this world and their part in it that they can be easily duped into believing the idealists. There always will be the unscrupulous Deceivers who are willing and able to use the fodder provided by the idealists and the ignorant to consolidate power, use it for their own purposes, and lord it over the masses. Fortunately, there also always will be the Washingtons, Adamses, Jeffersons, Hamiltons, Franklins, and Muhlenburgs who shall be possessed of "a firm reliance on the Protection of Divine Providence" and who will "mutually pledge to each other [their] Lives, [their] Fortunes, and [their] sacred Honor" to fight ignorance and malevolence and to defend for all mankind the unalienable, individual rights that were "endowed by their Creator." It has been rightly observed, however, that an ounce of prevention is worth a pound of cure. Therefore, at the same time we commit to cut back the federal government, let us also commit and plan to deny its resurgence. It is far better to prevent the causes of revolution than to fight one.

We have already alluded to an extremely effective way to contain the federal behemoth: we take control of the purse strings. Remember, whoever controls the purse strings controls the nose ring. Right now the federal government and its minions are in control of the purse strings, and they use them to lead us around like a cash cow. They pass laws to maintain their power, and then they pay for these laws either by taxing us (hurting us now) or by going further into debt (hurting us later). Let us turn the tables. Control their allowance and you control them.

First of all we must limit the supply of federal revenue to a single source, such as income tax or a national sales tax. The only exceptions to this rule would be compensation to the government for actual services rendered – like issuing a passport or granting a copyright – and punitive fines for non-compliance with the law – like a percentage surcharge on delinquent tax payments. This restriction on the sources of federal revenue **must** be implemented if there is to be any hope of controlling the purse strings. The Deceivers have proved to be very creative in coming up with imaginative, new ways to separate us from our earnings. Let's look at a few examples: individual income taxes, corporate income taxes, cigarette taxes, excise taxes, unemployment taxes, gasoline taxes, Social Security taxes, Medicare taxes, liquor taxes, estate taxes, telephone taxes, plus a rash of other taxes imposed at the state and local levels – and almost none of them existed one hundred years ago. If we do not limit federal revenue to a single source, then the Deceivers will simply add new sources and use the money to keep growing the government.

Limiting the flow of federal revenue to a single source is a good start, but there are other restrictions which must be implemented. We also must impose a cap to this levy, and we must forbid the federal government from going into debt. Failure to require all of these restrictions will simply leave too many escape hatches through which the Deceivers may easily slither. To illustrate how this would work, let's assume that we decided upon a national income tax as the single source of federal revenue; and since this book is titled *Solutions*, I will offer a very specific plan for funding the federal government while preventing its growth to unhealthy and unsafe levels in the future.

A flat tax in the range of 10 to 15 percent is imposed on the income of all individuals. There are no exemptions, deductions, nor sliding scales. Pick a percent – it applies to everyone. Whether you make $10,000 or $1,000,000 a year, you pay the same rate, let's say 15%. (Actually, statistics indicate that we could fund the federal government very generously at a much lower rate – probably in the vicinity of 9.5% or lower; but I don't want to be accused of creating a self-serving strawman, so I will use 15% for this illustration.) Some of my readers are outraged right now – probably the same ones who have been bilious all along. You demand, "How fair is it to make someone who earns only $10,000 a year pay the same rate as someone who makes $1,000,000?!?" Did you ever stop to consider how fair it is to make one of these people pay $150,000 while the other pays only $1,500? The millionaire does not derive one hundred times the benefits from his tax dollars as does the "ten-thousandaire." You're right, the system I propose *is* unfair, but not to the one making only $10,000. It is unfair to the one making $1,000,000, but I can live with that until a better suggestion comes along.

Others of you may take exception to the proposal for no deductions. "What about married couples, dependents, donations to charities, set-asides for pensions, and healthcare costs?!? What about those?!?" What about them? They are all personal decisions that persons should be able to make based upon the merits of a particular course of action and not upon the tax consequences associated with that course of action. Remember, we are returning to a system where the people may pursue life, liberty, and happiness as they see fit. We no longer are going to encourage social re-engineering by political ideologues who use governmental power to steer social and personal behavior in a direction they favor. You will be taxed simply to pay for your share of the collective costs associated with giving you "a more perfect union, establish justice, insure domestic tranquility, provide for the common defense, promote the general welfare, and secure the blessings of liberty to ourselves and our pos-terity." (By the way, let me throw a bone to all my left-leaning objectors: You might want to remember that I said, "We no longer are going to encourage social re-engineering" when we get to the portion about building a moral society. I'm sure you are going to want to throw that remark back in my face. Just a helpful hint; or, is it a trap?)

We also should forbid all income taxes on businesses – corporate or otherwise. I know, I know; now I'm "a heart-less, pro-business lackey who seeks to sacrifice the interests of working men and women on the cold, hard altar of corporate profits." Ooh, that really hurt, but did you ever stop to think what profits are spent on – whether from a corporation, LLC, partnership, or proprietorship?

For one thing, bigger profits create the opportunity for the entire workforce to make more money. Beyond that, some of the profits are invested. This investment creates job security and the potential for enhanced wages and salaries to those who have jobs and new employment possibilities for those who do not have jobs. And, of course, profits also provide the opportunity for all those celebrated bonuses, dividends, and luxurious corporate salaries that incense the rest of us. But even these are generally used to buy something or invest in something that creates more jobs and more wealth. Ultimately profits benefit everyone, and the bigger the profits the bigger the benefits.

You must understand that the Deceivers have a vested interest in class war, or at least class envy and strife. They use it to justify raising taxes which go to finance their schemes and to perpetuate their power. For example, we often hear about adding to the tax burden of the rich or, conversely, about denying the wealthy tax cuts that are proposed for others. How do you justify this? Why is the government entitled to take away even more money from wealthy people than it already does? Does it cost the government more to keep them around? No! In fact, they contribute far more per capita to government revenue and the economy in general than the rest of us. The only reason the "reformers" can talk about (1) raising the taxes of the wealthy or (2) denying them tax cuts that are granted to others is because no one has much sympathy for the rich. We are inclined to be jealous of their good fortune and their great fortunes, and the "reformers" are careful to keep this class envy simmering. Let me be clear: I abhor the opulent lifestyle as well as the twitty, self-aggrandizing mentality of those who crave that lifestyle, but I do not begrudge them the choice to spend their money as they choose; nor do I think we are entitled to take away from them even more of what they have earned just because we may be a bit jealous. That seems rather twitty also. The rest of us lowlanders would be well-advised to remember that the greed of the super-rich drives them to invest in all those activities that give the rest of us a job and a much higher standard of living than we would have had without them.

The simple fact is this: in a free-market economy virtually every penny of wealth that we have available to us originally came from the operation of a business. Some may object saying, "But I work for the government. My paycheck didn't come from a business." Yes, it did. Follow the money trail. The government doesn't create wealth; it seizes it. The paycheck of every government employee was funded by the proceeds of a business. Virtually all true wealth originally comes from the operation of some business – whether it's Bob's hotdog cart down there in the plaza or the multi-national corporation that has a suite of offices overlooking Bob's enterprise – it is business that stokes the engines of the economy. To take a hostile posture toward business makes about as much sense as strangling the goose that lays the golden eggs.

If you haven't gotten the point yet, let me try another illustration. Taxing businesses makes about as much sense as stealing gasoline from your own gas tank. We rely on our cars to take us places we want to go, but the less fuel we have the fewer places we can go. Stealing from your own gas tank only hurts you. Similarly, we rely on our businesses to create the wealth – goods and services – that enrich us all. Anything which makes our businesses less productive makes us less wealthy – and not just the wealthy, **all** of us. Taxing our businesses hurts us all.

So far we have discussed the requirement to restrict the revenue of the federal government to a single source. There remain three other things which must be done to effectively corral our profligate politicians. First, we also **must** strictly limit the government's ability to draw from that source, otherwise the Deceivers will acquire more and more revenue simply by changing the percentage that is owed to them. We accomplish this by legally limiting what the government may take to a specific percentage of revenue – like X% of income if we choose income tax, or Y% of sales if we choose a national sales tax. Yet even this action can be easily outflanked by the Deceivers and charlatans unless we also take a second step: we forbid the federal government from going into debt. If we neglect this the politicians simply will keep spending even after they have exhausted their income. They have been doing it for decades. We have no reason to expect them to change.

There is still a third major precaution which we must take to prevent being out-maneuvered by the big spenders. We must require the federal government to fully fund all its mandates from its own financial resources. As the tax burden has grown, the big spenders have heard Americans moan. I'm not sure just how sympathetic the Deceivers and charlatans are to the suffering of the taxpayers, but I am quite sure that they fear a taxpayer revolt. So they found a way to continue their campaign of social re-engineering while sparing the taxpayer – at least so it seemed. They passed laws which benefited a particular constituency but mandated that these benefits be paid by someone other than the taxpayer. In effect they create a non-monetary entitlement, which still is very costly to the populace – just in a less visible way. An example is the Americans with Disabilities Act. While waving the flag of making society more accessible to the handicapped – something only a moral monster could oppose – they required the costs of implementing the law to be borne, not by taxpayers but by another segment of the society. Guess who. Businesses, of course. Uncounted billions of dollars have been spent retrofitting existing structures – which met construction codes when they were first built – in order to install ramps at precisely the right gradient, rip out old doors and install new ones a few inches wider, and make sure the center of toilets were a minimum of eighteen inches from the wall – along with a myriad of other structural and non-structural requirements. These mandates strangled – in some cases to death – thousands of businesses while creating a boon for ambulance-chasing (or in this case, wheelchair-chasing) attorneys, some of whom sent out handicapped individuals looking for any infractions so they could make a lucrative income by suing business owners for non-compliance. (I suppose it is a mere coincidence that there are more lawyers in Congress than there are members from any other profession.)

This tactic was ingenious from the big-spenders' perspective, and once again we see malevolence and ignorance ally to form a masterful tag team. The Deceivers and charlatans bought themselves another constituency: the disabled. What was even better, the taxpayer generally took no offense because they didn't see their taxes go up one whit as a result of the new law. (There were some minor hits on government funds in order to pay for some retrofitting of government facilities – but nothing so significant that anyone really noticed.) Sadly, few taxpayers stopped to think that they also are consumers, and almost anything that causes the cost of business to go up will also cause an increase in the cost of the goods and services purchased from those businesses. So, while John and Jane Public were carefully guarding their right pocket, the politicians were skillfully picking the left one. Just more smoke and mirrors by the Deceivers – which is how they earned their richly deserved name. If the taxpayer had clearly seen up front how much it would cost him to pay for these measures, he might have thought twice about how dear they were to him. (I know, I know – I'm a heartless monster again. Well, allow me to round out your perspective. Both my parents spent more than the last decade of their lives significantly disabled and substantially limited in their mobility. I logged uncounted miles strolling along beside them steadying their walkers or behind them propelling their wheelchairs. And although I would have given whatever I could to alleviate their condition, I never expected anyone else to.)

Let us summarize. Once we have surgically removed the lard from the federal government by ceasing the entitlement programs mentioned, we must prevent the government from returning to obesity with a simple, four-part policy:

1. Revenue for the federal government are limited to a single source.
2. A fixed cap is placed on the amount which the federal government can take from this source.
3. The federal government may not go into debt.
4. The federal government must fully fund all its mandates from its own revenue.

Such a policy will force the federal government to carefully consider its priorities because it will no longer be able to respond to the question, "How much of this stuff should we do?" with the answer, "Why not all of it?" The government will have to live within its means just like the rest of us, and that means making tough choices. There is, however, one more important consideration. Even the best-run and happiest of nations will from time to time face extraordinary and costly emergencies; for example the devastation of natural mega-disasters or the demands of fighting a righteous war. It is easy to imagine that the costs of dealing with these emergencies will exceed the funds available under the formula offered above. Accordingly, we must have an emergency exemption available to the government so it can respond to true emergencies in a responsible manner. For this reason we will permit the federal government to raise the fixed cap on taxation (mentioned in Number 2 above) under the following conditions:

1. The amount of the increase is specifically designated and not open-ended (for example, raising the individual income tax from fifteen percent to seventeen percent).

2. The additional revenue may only be spent on the purpose for which they were designated, like disaster relief or wartime expenditures.

3. The increase has a "Sunset Clause"; in other words, it expires after a certain period of time, like two or three years. At that time the rate of taxation reverts to the previous level.

4. The above terms must be submitted in a plebiscite (a yes or no vote) to all eligible voters and approved by a super-majority of sixty-five percent. The requirement for a super-majority is essential. Without it the Deceivers and charlatans can pursue new ambitions anytime they happen to muster the support of a mere majority of the people. This requirement also insures that a

substantial portion of the nation is in agreement as to the worthiness of these expenditures.

By controlling the funds available to the federal government, we control the growth of the federal government and force our government officials to make responsible decisions. Whenever one has to deal with a "necessary evil", it is wise to insure that it is kept on a short leash and well shackled. I believe that adopting the restrictions detailed above will go a long way toward accomplishing this.

CHAPTER SIX

PAYDAY vs. PAYDAY

Before we go on to consider some unique solutions to specific problems facing the nation, let us consider another aspect of reforming the systemic problem of big government: What happens to paychecks when you go from a system of collective responsibility managed by the government (the Nanny-State) to a system of individual responsibility managed by the individual?

I have proposed the nearly total elimination of the entitlement programs administered by the federal government. This, in turn, would cut the federal budget by more than half and drastically reduce the size and intrusiveness of government. I have also proposed a way to prevent the federal government from growing back, like some weed that merely has been pruned instead of pulled up by the roots. This will not eliminate all our woes – there always will be troubles – but it will eliminate the worst of those woes which have been created or aggravated by the federal government. An essential element of this reform consists of returning to a lifestyle that emphasizes individual responsibility as opposed to collective responsibility. Now, let's get real. Let's not talk vaguely about the blessings of greater personal liberty; let's see exactly what this will do for you personally by looking at the effect this will have on your paycheck.

Actually, I must confess that I cannot accomplish this as "exactly" as I would like. The payroll system established and perpetuated by the various levels of government is so twisted and complicated that it is impossible to "exactly" show how my system will affect your take-home pay. Paychecks are impacted by such variables as the number of dependents and deductions and variable income tax rates and Social Security and Medicare and 401K's and IRA's and company-managed pensions and health insurance and educational savings accounts and whether you drive a "green" car and … and … and…. Because of this it is impossible to give a single figure or percentage that is deducted from everyone's earnings. I cannot do this, but you can. Look at your payroll stub or payment record. See how much you earned (gross income) and see how much you actually received after all the deductions (net income). If you like, divide your net income (the small amount) by the gross income (the big amount). The answer is the percentage you actually get to keep. (Let's say your gross income for a pay-period was $1,500 and your net pay, after all the deductions, was $1,095. $1,095 divided by $1,500 is .73, or 73%.) Subtract that percentage from 100 and that is the percentage you lose because of all the deductions.

(100 minus 73 equals 27, so the total deductions in this example add up to 27% of gross income.)

Ah, if only it were that simple. There's more. You cost your employer far more than your gross wage or salary. There are a variety of other expenses which the boss has to pay but which probably do not show up on your pay stub – things like worker's compensation insurance and employer contributions to a variety of other taxes and benefits like FICA and FUTA and SUTA and health insurance and pension, etc. Here again, there simply are too many variables for me to predict how much these costs add up to in your case. Worker's compensation rates, for example, vary considerably depending on whether you are a secretary or a roofer. However, accountants and payroll specialists with whom I have consulted generally agree that these additional employer expenses can be expected to add a minimum of 12% to 15% to the total cost of an employee. A more likely range would be between 25% and 30%. So, using our earlier example of someone who grosses $1,500, the actual cost of that employee to the employer would be $1,875 – and that's if we use the lower amount of 25%. (To find out what your actual cost is to your employer, just ask; or to get a ballpark figure, take your gross income and multiply it times 1.25 – again assuming the smaller amount of 25%.)

So, let's assume that you were the mythical employee mentioned above – the one who grosses $1,500 but only gets to take home $1,095. Under my plan you would gross the entire amount of $1,875 because we would eliminate all the deductions except one: the federal income tax mentioned in the previous chapter. Even if we assume that tax to be on the high side of the range I suggested – 15% – your take-home pay would be $1,593.75. I just gave you a 45.5% raise! Now, don't be too quick to thank me, because my plan also took away all your government and business and union administered benefits. You must understand, however, that putting the government or your employer or your union in charge of all this money is a tactic (would "scam" be too harsh of a word?) to give them power and to take it away from you. Why should your pension or healthcare be dependent upon the integrity and competence of the government or your employer or your union? Think of all the people who have lost their pensions and health insurance because of the incompetence of a boss or union – and we're all getting cheated by the government. Why should you have to wait years before you are vested in a retirement program – years during which someone else gets the use of your money? Why should you lose your health insurance because you move or change jobs? We have constructed a system where control of some of the most important aspects of your life – like a secure retirement and your healthcare – is taken from you and given to another, namely the government or an employer or a union. Why? Power. Remember, whoever controls the purse strings controls the nose ring; and right now your boss and your union and your government have set up a system whereby they can lead you around and have you dance to their tunes. They get the sweet, secure pensions and the Cadillac healthcare policies while you worry about whether you will still be covered tomorrow. Forget that! Change the system and take back control! Everything that is currently being provided by the government and companies and unions can be acquired by you through private companies. Furthermore, such a change would create huge new opportunities for job growth in the private sector. Think of all the private sector growth that would take place if private companies were permitted to do what only the government is doing now. You could still have unemployment insurance and worker's compensation insurance and health insurance and an excellent pension program – all through the private sector, which tends to be much more efficient and less wasteful than the public sector, which means you get more bang for your buck. And please don't be so bone-headed as to reply, "Why should I agree to your plan where I have to pay for everything? Right now my boss pays for it." No, he doesn't. **YOU DO**! All these things you think your boss is paying for are costs of labor, and YOU are the laborer. I want YOU to get ALL the costs of labor, and I want to allow YOU to spend it as YOU see fit – not as your boss or your union official or a government bureaucrat sees fit. YOU earned it. Why do you allow THEM to control it and you? Frankly, if you object to the system I just proposed, you don't deserve the title, "American." It was hard-working, self-sufficient, self-reliant, liberty-loving, government-spurning people who built this nation and made it great. Get on the bandwagon or get off the bus.

PART TWO

SPECIFIC ISSUES

CHAPTER SEVEN

CRIME: ISLAND LIFE

Immediately before I turn in for the night I check the six locks on the three doors that lead into the house. Several windows have stickers which boast the name of a prominent alarm system; and within easy reach of the bed are "friends" ever-ready to help me greet any uninvited visitors who may somehow venture unwelcomed into our personal castle. And we live in a relatively safe neighborhood. The "grannies", on the other hand, would tell a different tale – a serene story of unlocked doors, opened windows, and peace. Times have changed and not for the better. From pinheads who can't think of any better way to define themselves than by defacing someone else's property with a can of spray paint to monsters who showcase their demonic obsessions by exterminating entire families with personal weapons of mass destruction, crime in America has become more commonplace and more savage. We will talk about changing the moral foundation of America later. Surely the best way to reduce crime is by inculcating a personal code of conduct which makes the very thought of such deviant behavior reprehensible and far beneath one's personal dignity. Rebuilding a moral America and moral Americans, however, will take a while. In the meantime we need to do something that will have a much more immediate effect.

First, pause a moment to consider the cost-benefit ratio of our penal system. As a nation we expend far too many valuable resources incarcerating "lost causes." On a spiritual level I like to think that there is no such thing as a "lost cause." As a society, however, it is safe to say that anyone who has been sentenced to "twenty-five years to life" or worse can be officially considered a "lost cause." Now, think how much it costs us to maintain these losses. It is not uncommon for the citizens of a state to pay upwards of thirty or even forty thousand dollars a year per inmate to cage these reprobates. Hundreds to thousands of security personnel are diverted from more productive employment and instead are used to insure that the convicts stay where we put them. The prisoners themselves are supplied, at taxpayers' expense, with nutritious meals and health care and recreation rooms and televisions and libraries and exercise equipment and internet and … and … and…. They often live better than many of their victims, except for the matter of personal freedom. Why? Why do we expend so many valuable resources on so many lost causes when there are so many hopeful causes to support?

Before considering a specific proposal to address the problems of crime and criminals, let us first remember a basic condition upon which all community living depends. Throughout the ages many great socio-political thinkers have referred, in one way or another, to a concept often called the "social contract." Put simply it states that whenever two or more people live in association with one another, there must be some ground rules to govern their behavior.

We are told that no man is an island – a solitary being living a solitary existence. If such a being existed – like the proverbial shipwrecked sailor on a deserted island – he would have no need for laws nor contracts to regulate his personal behavior, for his actions would never affect the life of another. He could do whatever he chose with no social consequences. However, as soon as two or more individuals begin to interact, the behavior of each individual now has the potential to affect the others. Some guidelines must be developed to insure that a measure of harmony and mutual gain results from that social interaction, otherwise a perpetual state of war could result.

Political philosophers and their chroniclers have filled volumes describing what really is a pretty simple idea. The essence of the social contract is an agreement to scratch someone else's back as long as they scratch yours; and should someone ever stop scratching your back, we, collectively, will make them rue the day they decided to keep their hands in their pockets. What generally

63

happens when a community is formed is that each of the parties to this community agrees to surrender some measure of personal freedom in exchange for some desired benefits which will be shared by all the parties in the community. Usually the benefit is a greater degree of peace and security. This "deal" among the parties is the "social contract." As long as the parties adhere to the contract, they all may derive the benefits of their collective interaction. However, there inevitably are those who will break the terms of the contract, usually for selfish reasons. They seek some personal gain which exceeds what they could normally expect by honoring the terms of the code. This gain, however, is usually acquired at the expense of others in the community. Those "others" often feel abused and cheated. Their interests have been harmed; they are personally offended; and they often will seek retribution. The consequences of this errant behavior can be very destabilizing to the community, for it threatens the system of mutual benefits that is the glue holding the society together. Accordingly, there must be some consequence which discourages this errant behavior. If not, the contract – and the society which benefits from its enforcement – will be in danger of collapsing.

Let us look at a simple and familiar example to illustrate how this works: the tenant / landlord relationship. The tenant desires an asset which he cannot afford; let's say a house in which to live. The landlord has an asset (again, let's say a house) from which he hopes to derive some income. So long as they remain isolated from each other they both lose. The tenant has no home. The landlord has no income. Once they are united, however, they both can achieve their goals so long as they both agree to make certain personal sacrifices. The tenant gains a house, but he loses the use of some money. The landlord gains some money, but he loses the use of the house. The two parties negotiate a social contract (lease) defining mutually agreeable terms. The tenant gets a place to live and the landlord secures some income. The agreement defines various terms and conditions to insure that the relationship does not become abusive to either party. For example, the landlord promises that the house is in good condition and he agrees to keep it that way so long as it wasn't the tenant who damaged the house, in which case the tenant will pay for repairs. The tenant agrees to pay a certain amount to the landlord at given intervals as compensation for the landlord providing a place to live. Neither side gets everything it wants (the tenant would like to have the house for no charge; the landlord would like to have twice as much rent), but so long as both parties honor the agreed-to conditions of the lease, there is peace and mutual benefit. However, as we said earlier, one party or the other occasionally attempts to break the agreement, which abuses the interests of the other. Both the offended party and the society in general have an interest in enforcing the contract (lease). Accordingly, if the tenant stops paying rent, he can be kicked out of the house. If the landlord fails to keep the house in livable condition, he can be forced to make the necessary repairs and pay a penalty for breaking the agreement.

Obviously, the rules (or social contract) for a larger society will be much more comprehensive and complex than those for a two-party community like the one just described. Still, all the general principles apply: the parties to the contract agree to make certain personal sacrifices in order to gain some personal and social benefits. Those who break the rules must be punished in order to prevent the breakdown of the society and all the benefits which it provides.

Now, let us return to the criminal and what to do about him. Criminals, by definition, have broken the terms of the social contract. Whether it is spray-painting a stranger's wall or slaughtering an innocent family, the criminal is in violation of the terms and conditions by which we all agree to live. The society must respond aggressively in order to keep the peace and security that people expect for the sacrifices they make to be a part of the community. In the case of lesser crimes, the goals of this social response should be to provide restitution to the offended party, reform the criminal (that is, to convince him that he should never again commit the crime), and to keep others from following the criminal's bad example (by making sure the punishment is severe and inevitable enough to be a deterrent). In the case of serious crimes, however, the society's objectives will change. Restitution may still be a goal, but since we can no longer trust the serious criminal to behave civilly, we have no interest in preparing him for re-entry into the society. Our only interest is to prevent him from ever again having the opportunity to victimize and terrorize innocents. By his own conduct he has, in effect, "voted himself off the island", and the rest of us want to insure that he can never return.

Given this objective of preventing the criminal from victimizing the civil population in the future, it is clear to see how irrational our current policy is of long-term incarceration. One way or another the criminal is put in a position to perpetuate the suffering of the general populace. There always remains a chance that the convict could escape; and given his predilections, he almost certainly will return to a life of crime thereby creating new victims. However, even if he should never again see the outside of the prison, the taxpayer is victimized by the significant costs associated with warehousing the inmates.

I propose that we embrace the concept of a prison colony for our worst criminals; that is, capital and near-capital offenders. I will refer to this colony as "Life Island." Life Island could be either a true island surrounded by a large body of water or a conceptual island isolated and insulated from the general populace by a large expanse of easily monitored land. To simplify and shorten our discussion, let us imagine that we are going to use a true island in the middle of an ocean or other large body of water. The island would be uninhabited except by the criminals sentenced there. Only criminals from one gender would be sentenced to this island – no co-ed incarceration. There would be no guards nor other support personnel on the island. The island would be habitable, though. There would be sources of fresh water and food – or at least the wherewithal to grow food, hunt, or fish. Convicts sentenced to Life Island would be delivered by a security patrol. Once the prisoners are dropped off at the island, civilized society will have no further contact with them. The inmates would be "free" to set up their own living arrangements, both individual and social. They could form and join tribes or go it alone. The only continuing cost to society would be the cost of security patrols to guard against escapes. If the colony were a true island, the security patrols could be incorporated into training exercises conducted by the Navy and Coast Guard. If the colony were on a deserted section of terrain, security patrols could be conducted by a combination of local, state, and federal police agencies or, again, incorporated into training exercises conducted by the Army and Marines.

Would such a prisoner lifestyle likely become barbaric? Almost certainly. But so, too, is the prisoner lifestyle in conventional penitentiaries. And so, too, is the civilian lifestyle when innocents become the victims of these barbarians. Under the Life Island concept, the barbarity is more effectively limited to the barbarians – which seems eminently more fair than the current situation.

What about the Constitutional restriction against administering punishments that are cruel and unusual?

Granted, this notion of Life Island is rather unique, although other prison colonies of a similar nature have been employed. Essentially, this is merely a modern version of the age-old practice of exile. But even if we do concede that this concept may be unusual for America, the Constitutional prohibition is against punishments that are both cruel **and** unusual. The framers deliberately used the word "and" not "or", and with good reason. Had they used the word "or" we never would be able to take advantage of any new forms of punishment and rehabilitation. So, even if we concede that this idea may be somewhat unusual, we would still have to consider how cruel it is. So, let's do that. Is it cruel to require our worst criminals to live the way that most humans have lived for the greatest part of our history and the way that many around the world still live? It may be primitive, but hardly cruel. Furthermore, we would have to ask how cruel it is to give someone his freedom and the only price he has to pay is to live with others like himself. Harsh? Yes. Cruel? Hardly. You see, the society is imposing no cruelty nor even any misery upon the convict. Any miseries associated with existence on Life Island would be created by the inhabitants themselves and not inflicted by the state, so we escape any Constitutional disqualifiers.

The adoption and implementation of this concept by itself would hardly eliminate crime in America or even significantly reduce it. It would make society safer, and it would make our penal system far less expensive.

My principal interest in it, however, is because it constitutes a crucial cornerstone in a crime-fighting approach
which **would** have a dramatic impact on reducing crime
in America. It is this approach which we will be considering in the next chapter.

CHAPTER EIGHT

DRUGS: PUT IT BACK

In the summer of 1970 I reported to Quantico, Virginia, for Marine officer training. Quite honestly, it was a scary experience. Hardly any of us knew anybody else in the platoon; we had little idea of what to expect other than the certainty of misery; we were being prepared to fight in the jungles of Vietnam; but all of that paled before the greatest and most immediate danger of all: the Marine Drill Instructor! These were the invincible ones – certain descendants of the Mighty Men spoken of in hushed and reverent voices in Biblical accounts. They needed no sleep. They saw everything. They could march for miles without breaking a sweat while both the temperature and the humidity were in the high nineties. They were the masters of every profane expression known to human-kind, for, in fact, they had conceived most of them. They had memorized verbatim the Marquis De Sade's hand-book on the methodology of exquisite torture, and they had no qualms about using everything they had learned.

Enlisted boot and officer candidate alike live in terror of – the D.I.

It was only the second or third day after we had reported in. We had already learned that "sleep" was something other people did. Our only sustenance was terror-induced adrenaline. On this particular afternoon we found ourselves herded into – and melting into – a grassy area between some quonset huts. We were once again waiting for something – I no longer recall what. No one was allowed to speak. And then it happened. Without warning one of the candidates decided to spit on the grass. Suddenly, time and space split asunder. In a nanosecond, and out of nowhere, there appeared a D.I. nose-to-nose with the doomed, would-be "butter-bars" ("second lieutenant" for you uninitiated). Everyone's heart seized and turned to stone within his chest. We cringed and braced for the inevitable, ear-splitting tirade. But there was none. The D.I. locked the candidate with a steely stare. The poor boy already knew he was a dead man standing. An infinity passed in just a few seconds, and then the D.I. spoke forcefully but calmly in that gravelly, guttural voice that seemed to be standard issue at D.I. school. "You spit on the Colonel's grass." The candidate had locked himself into an exaggerated position of attention. His eyes bulged, betraying the fear that inflamed every cell of his being. He said nothing. Speech, indeed, was impossible in such a condition. He simply nodded. The D.I., head tucked down like a ram ready to butt the object of his attention into the next week, simply said, "Put it back."

A shiver of horror coursed through all of us within ear-shot of the Drill Instructor's directive. Somehow, the candidate's eyes opened even farther. He blinked – twice – then looked downward at the slimy wad shimmering atop the blades of dark, green grass. An appeal was useless, and hesitation would only provoke a response from the Marquis' tome on sadistic pleasures. He swallowed hard, bent down, scooped up the phlegmy goo between his fingers, paused ever-so-briefly, and then he – put it back. The D.I. waited until he saw the forlorn jarhead swallow again, at which time he pivoted smartly and moved to a new perch awaiting his next victim.

The point of this story is not to gross-out the reader. The point is this: I don't ever remember again seeing another Marine spit, except far out in the field. Undoubtedly the Drill Instructors were taught to extinguish this crude behavior as soon as it manifested itself – and it worked. ***Effective punishment quickly and consistently applied works***. That is the lesson of this saliva-soaked story. Unfortunately, we, as individuals and as a society, seem either to have forgotten this lesson or to take such exception to it that we no longer implement it very effectively. This, in turn, is a big reason why we experience so much immoral, anti-social, and criminal behavior. Spare the rod and spoil – everything. You get the behavior you tolerate. That's the bad news. The good news is that you also get the behavior you insist upon. Example: in nearly a quarter of a century in the classroom, I never had a student fail a class – not one – and my standards were higher than the norm. Why? Simple. I insisted that my students perform, and I supervised every step to insure that they did. It wasn't easy for either of us, but when is anything truly worthwhile ever easy?

The application of this lesson to crime in America is obvious. Effective punishments quickly and consistently applied must be a part of our crime-fighting arsenal. To be sure, there are many other things which we must do as well, but this is probably the tactic that we can implement the fastest and from which we can start to see the quickest results. Now, let's get specific.

At the present time illegal drugs are a root cause for much of the crime we experience. The impact of this personal and social addiction reaches far beyond the number of people who produce, sell, and use drugs. Drug use provokes a great many other criminal and destructive behaviors. Much of the thievery that takes place (robbery, burglary, muggings, home invasions, embezzlement, car-jackings, etc.) is committed by those looking for ways to finance their addiction. The growth and power of gangs is fueled by the income derived from the sale of drugs. Drug use alters personal behavior in a variety of baleful ways. It provokes some to violence while others sink into lethargy. Jobs are lost, families are destroyed, and the future is forsaken. Solve the drug problem and we will solve a great deal of what is plaguing this nation.

How do we do this? For the most immediate results we simply must remember the rule, "***Effective punishment quickly and consistently applied works***." Here is my solution.

Everyone who is convicted of using illegal drugs will be sentenced to ten years in prison plus a $100,000 fine – ***unless*** he informs on his supplier. ***If*** the convict provides credible testimony that results in the conviction of the supplier, the sentence is reduced to six months of prison or rehabilitation (according to the best judgment of the court) and a $5,000 fine. Now think about it. What druggie wouldn't rat out his supplier in order to get back nine-and-a-half years of his life and $95,000 of income? I dare say not many. In a single stroke we just created an army of very well-motivated informants who will eagerly assist the police in sweeping the drug dealers off the streets. And where will these vermin be swept? You don't think I wrote Chapter Seven for nothing, do you? ***Everyone*** convicted of being involved in any part of the drug business – growing, producing, financing, transporting, selling, facilitating, whatever – will be sentenced to Life Island. Period.

Now, let us consider the impact of such a policy. Current drug users will have a considerable incentive to stop using. If they do, great. We just took a big bite out of the problem, and there is less demand for this pernicious product thereby making the business of illegal drugs less tempting. On the other hand, if current users persist, sooner or later they will get caught and will face the option of losing either ten years of their life and $100,000 or six months of their life and $5,000.

I suspect most will choose what's behind Door Number Two – in fact, they will jump at it. On the supply side of the problem, those in the business will soon realize that their freedom depends upon the loyalty of pot-heads, glue-sniffers, snow-noses, and a collection of other junkies. Not a good bet. Hopefully, many will leave the business and find more productive pursuits. If they don't, not to worry – they soon will be on their way to a perennial appointment on Life Island. The risk-to-return calculations for those in the business will significantly shift to the risk side of the equation, and fewer will find it worth taking the chance.

Some variations on this theme could be considered. For example, a small-time street dealer might be offered a long-term alternative to Life Island if he provides credible testimony leading to the conviction of a higher-up in the drug business.

Never underestimate the creativity of an errant spirit. Some users who may still have enough brain cells remaining to have a creative thought may be thinking that they can avoid the worst consequences of this policy by growing or making their own supplies. Sorry, that falls under the category of being "in the business." Off to Life Island with you.

Another benefit of this plan is that it would breathe new life into those law enforcement officials who have lost their motivation to pursue the "Little Guy." I have talked with a number of police officers and sheriff's deputies who say that it just isn't worth their while to pursue the small-timers. The "system" is so lenient and so over-whelmed that it is a waste of time – nothing of conse-quence is achieved. Under the plan just described, even the arrest of someone with a mere ounce of marijuana could have a significant impact on fighting drugs since it could very easily take a dealer – or worse – off the street.

Illegal drugs destroy lives, families, communities, and nations. The problem is already epidemic and threaten-ing to get much worse. The rise of very powerful and very violent drug cartels has only increased the urgency for attacking and destroying this problem immediately. Like a cancerous tumor, the best time to address the disease is before it becomes too deeply rooted. Unfortunately, that time has passed, which means that a cure will not come easily nor without scars, but it must come or all could be lost. ***Effective punishment quickly and consistently applied works***. We've wasted too much time and too many lives with lenient attitudes and weak responses. If we continue to spare the rod, we will spoil – everything.

CHAPTER NINE

ILLEGAL IMMIGRATION: JU JITSU

A plaque mounted inside the pedestal of the Statue of Liberty recites a poem written by Emma Lazarus. That poem contains these famous words, "Give me your tired, your poor, your huddled masses yearning to breathe free…." The prospects of freedom, prosperity, and a new life have attracted people to this land even before the founding of the United States. The phenomenal success of this country has only added to that attraction. As the slogan "E pluribus unum" ("out of many, one") suggests, we are a nation of many nations. This diversity has both inspired greatness and provoked problems, but overall it has been a great blessing. Still, like any other challenge, this, too, must be well-managed or the problems will soon outweigh and overshadow the blessings. Truly, we are a nation of immigrants, but immigration itself must be controlled or we endanger the very thing the immigrants seek. A lifeboat also offers the prospect of new life, but if too many climb aboard, the whole vessel will sink and all will be lost.

The immigration policies of a nation must have as their primary objective the overall well-being of that nation and its people. A desire to help everyone everywhere is very noble, but there is only so much that any one person or nation can accomplish. Trying to do too much can destroy one's ability to do anything. Whereas the compassionate heart knows no limits, the cardiac muscle does. Overwork it and it dies. We must pace ourselves. As Abraham Lincoln is reputed to have said, "You cannot help the poor by destroying the rich. You cannot strengthen the weak by weakening the strong." If we do not preserve our ability to create wealth, there will be nothing that we can do for the poor. If we do not maintain our strength, there will be nothing that we can do to defend the weak.

Personally, I welcome the people of all races, nations, and religions to our shores – *__as long as they respect our laws__* – and this includes those laws governing how and how many people of other races, nations, and religions come to these shores. In recent decades there has been a great debate about how to handle the people who did not respect our laws when they entered this land. These people are called "illegal immigrants" because they immigrated here unlawfully. Not unexpectedly, politics and politicians have entered that debate and, predictably, that debate often has taken on some absurd characteristics. Take, for example, the proposal to give illegal immigrants driver's licenses or other forms of authentic identification. It seems to me that a key word in the expression "illegal immigrant" must be the word, "illegal." Regardless of their motivation for coming here, these people are breaking our law. Aiding and abetting a criminal is also breaking the law; and giving illegal immigrants official identification cards only makes it easier for them to continue breaking our laws. Maybe I'm nuts, but it seems to me that you don't give home invaders the key to your front door; you don't elect a pedophile to be president of the PTA; you don't give a serial rapist a membership to Match.com; and you don't give an illegal immigrant a driver's license or other form of identification. Another obvious absurdity is the establishment of "sanctuary cities" which promise not to act on the fact that a person is here illegally should that fact come to light. That makes about as much sense as telling bank robbers that we won't prosecute them if they can just make it to Cleveland before being caught. (No offense, Cleveland. I love you, but I had to pick someplace, and I figured you were strong enough to take it.) None of these practices make any sense, until you factor in the politician and his often-nefarious objectives. The politician, of course, pleads compassionate motives. However, if you scratch the thin, shiny veneer of compassion, you likely will find a bottomless cesspool of self-interest. In fact, the politician is likely trying to buy the votes and/or financial support of (1) the family, friends, and other members of the same national heritage as the illegal; (2) those who profit from the presence of illegals (which includes all manner of unscrupulous businessmen, human traffickers, drug dealers, and pimps); and (3) the illegals themselves, especially if they can hang around long enough to be blessed by the next grant of amnesty and become grateful voters.

Given the lifestyle of the illegal immigrant, it is difficult to assess the magnitude of the problems they present; indeed, some defenders even maintain that they represent a net gain to our economy. (Again, never underestimate the creativity of an errant spirit.) The situation is fluid and difficult to measure, but seemingly reliable estimates indicate that there are upwards of ten million illegal immigrants in the country and that their net economic cost to the society could be well over one hundred billion dollars annually – most of which is borne by the individual states, although perhaps twenty-five to thirty percent seems to be borne by the federal government. In fact, some estimates indicate that the amount spent by states like Texas and California on illegal immigrants is very close to or exceeds the total amount of those states' budget deficits. Whatever the actual numbers may be, few would dispute the claim that the costs are considerable. They manifest themselves in such ways as higher educational costs, medical expenses, humanitarian and welfare assistance, burdens on the police, judicial, and penitentiary systems, along with the costs associated with securing and patrolling the borders and deportation. There are also heavy social costs that accompany these economic ones. Not most, but a significant portion of the illegals who come here are involved in dangerous criminal activities which prey upon law-abiding Americans.

As indicated above, there are those who argue that the presence of the illegals actually contributes to a net gain in the society. We often hear these defenders make the claim that the illegals take the jobs that most Americans won't. To state that more correctly, we should say that the illegals take the jobs that many Americans ***don't have to*** because our exceedingly lenient and generous entitlement programs subsidize their slothful and unproductive lifestyles. Once these programs are eliminated, as proposed in Chapter Four, I think we can safely bet that many Americans will be clamoring for these jobs.

The operating assumption of this chapter is that the presence of a large illegal immigrant population in the United States is a significant problem and that it needs to be solved – something which is not happening now. So, what can we do differently that would make a difference? Ju Jitsu.

"Ju Jitsu" (or, perhaps more correctly, "Jujutsu") is a Japanese martial art that specializes in using no or minimal weaponry to defend oneself. Instead of brute force, the practitioner uses the assailant's own energy against him, rather than directly opposing it. For example, should an attacker come rushing toward you, don't go crashing into him headlong. Side-step the aggressor and, as he goes by, give him a little pull in the direction he already is heading. This will cause him to lose balance and fall face down, which gives the intended victim the opportunity to turn the tables. A similar principle can be used to stanch the flow of illegals into our country.

At the present time, and for quite some time now, the major source of illegal immigrants into the United States has been Latin America; and most of them have entered the United States by crossing the border with Mexico. The Mexican government has no real incentive to stop this. In fact, the Mexican government has a considerable incentive to permit and even encourage this flow of illegals into the United States. Mexico has its own social problems – problems which are alleviated by the significant numbers which leave Mexico and come here. The United States constitutes a "safety valve" for our friends to the south. Furthermore, illegals in the United States send millions of dollars to family members in Mexico, hurting our economy but helping theirs. (One authoritative source indicates that these "remittances" amount to just over two percent of Mexico's Gross Domestic Product.) Instead of continuing to spend a fortune on a variety of activities which consistently prove to be only minimally effective, I propose that we hire the Mexican government to prevent the problem before we have to solve it. (Remember that an ounce of prevention is worth a pound of cure.) Here's how it would work.

The federal government of the United States will offer the Mexican government a substantial amount of foreign aid annually – let's say twenty billion dollars, although that number is subject to debate. The money would be delivered sometime in the first half of each calendar year. There's just one catch: we will deduct one dollar from that amount for every dollar that we spend on dealing with the problem of illegal immigrants that came from or through Mexico. This would give the Mexican government a considerable incentive to solve the problem on their side of the border. I could be wrong, but I kind of think that with twenty billion dollars at stake they would be willing to post guards elbow-to-elbow along the border to insure that no one gets across. Our problem, though not completely solved (that never seems to happen and shouldn't be expected), is drastically alleviated and at a bargain price while the Mexican government gets some much-needed operating capital. Granted, it would be very Pollyannaish to expect them to use all that money honorably, but that's on their head, not ours. We will have made a substantial contribution that could be used to lessen Mexico's internal ills which, in turn, would make Mexico a much better place in which to live. Certainly it is far better to help Mexicans prosper in their own land than to have to travel – illegally and often dangerously – to a foreign land in order to scratch out a living.

Well, this proposal should help to dry up the flood of illegals entering our country in the future, but what about those who are already here? This ten-plus million population would continue to impose considerable costs upon our nation and, furthermore, those costs would be deducted from the twenty billion dollars that the Mexican government could potentially earn. That hardly seems fair, and it could lessen the incentive of Mexican officials to stem the tide in the future. To deal with the problem of the illegal immigrants who already are here I would propose amnesty – ah, but not the amnesty that you probably are thinking about. In the past "amnesty" has referred to granting citizenship, or at least legal residency, to those who are currently in the nation illegally. Basically, this amounts to rewarding law-breakers for having done an especially good job of not getting caught. This doesn't seem like a very wise policy to adopt nor precedent to establish. The amnesty I propose would work a little differently. We offer every illegal immigrant the chance to surrender within three months. For those who take this opportunity (1) we will return them to their homeland without cost, (2) we will give them two thousand dollars for each adult and one thousand dollars for every child, and (3) we will not pursue legal prosecution, unless they are wanted for having committed crimes other than being here illegally. On the other hand, if they choose to stay and are caught, they will be prosecuted and, upon conviction, receive a substantial prison sentence. Upon the conclusion of that sentence they will be deported without a penny. Harsh? Yes. Effective? Undoubtedly. And for our soft-headed as well as soft-hearted critics, keep in mind that the only thing that has to be done to avoid this harshness is simply to turn oneself in. Remember, these illegals are breaking our laws and draining resources from our own people. If they want to come to the United States, wonderful. ***Do it legally!***

In the meantime, they should work on making their own homeland a better place to live – which is exactly what we Americans did with our homeland. It works if you are willing to work.

Instead of trying to solve the problem of illegal immigration by butting heads with it like opposing linemen in the National Football League, let us use the natural energy of the situation to accomplish our goals, as in the art of Ju Jitsu. Use the desire of the Mexican government for much needed cash to stem the flow of illegal immigration. Use the desire of the illegal immigrant for much needed cash to motivate them to return home with a considerable down payment on their future. And let us use a tiny portion of the wealth generated by our considerable economic engines to accomplish these goals while saving us even more money in the future.

Win, win, win.

CHAPTER TEN

NATIONAL SERVICE: THE JEEP

A nation is more than a group of people who live within a specific geographic area and who share a common government. A nation takes on a life and identity of its own which is both given by the people and given back to the people. Different images and characteristics come to mind when we say "Chinese" and "French" and "Egyptian" and "Chilean" and "Samoan" and "American." Each of these people has defined themselves differently; and they are perceived as being different from other people both by themselves and by others. Individual identity is tied up with national identity – and vice versa. Similarly, individual security is tied up with national security – and vice versa. Each individual has an interest in supporting and defending his nation just as much as he has an interest in supporting and defending himself and his family; for, in fact, these are to a considerable degree inseparable. An individual cannot be truly secure if his nation is not. By the same token, a nation cannot be truly secure if its people are not. We spoke earlier about the need to protect the people from the inept, inefficient, misguided, debilitating, and often corrupt operations of government. Now it is time to flip the coin and speak of the people's obligation to serve the nation which serves them; for the fact is, we will get as we give.

In his inaugural address of January, 1961, President John Kennedy challenged the nation with these words, "Ask not what your country can do for you; ask what you can do for your country." Actually, we the people are very entitled to ask what our country can do for us. However, the collective entity which we call the "country" or the "nation" is also very entitled to ask what we individuals can do for it. In our modern-day society with its ferociously hedonistic tendencies, any thought of "what we can do for our country" is often given short shrift. "Honor" and "duty" are alien concepts to many people in our nation today. Their only thought of "serving" the country comes when they cannot find a good-paying civilian job and their unemployment benefits are about to run out. We all share an obligation to support and defend our nation, and we all should be proud to do so.

I just paused to think how I should phrase my next comment. As I did, my gaze drifted up to a painting which hangs on the wall behind my desk. I deliberately put it there so that I **must** see it and so that I **must** be reminded of its powerful message every day. It is a painting by Arnold Friberg. It depicts General George Washington kneeling in the snow at Valley Forge – praying. You can see his horse's breath, a chilling testimony not only of the winter that has descended upon the beleaguered troops huddled nearby, but also of the winter that has descended upon the hopes of the American cause. The Revolution itself is at stake. All Patriot eyes turn to General Washington – their only hope in this desperate hour. The General closes his eyes. He bends his knee, and he bows his head. His tri-corner hat lies beside him on the frozen ground. His hands are clutched, betraying the urgency of his appeal. The Patriot cause teeters on the brink of disaster. There is only one thing left to do – but the General has learned that this one thing is the most important thing that he must do to insure victory. He turns to God. He prays to "the beneficent Author of all the good that was, that is, or that will be." He prays for the rectitude of their cause and for Divine Providence to defend it.

The painting is based upon an eye-witness account of General Washington praying, alone, in the wintry woods of Pennsylvania. We can only imagine that upon concluding his appeal the General returned to his camp and looked at the troops whom he and God would rely upon to accomplish that prayer. It is no different today. The Revolution, again, is at stake. As did George Washington during the winter of 1777 – 1778, and on uncounted other occasions, we all need to pray; and then we all must not only await God's answer, we must answer it ourselves. We must come to the aid of our country. This is our heritage.

This is our legacy. This is our duty. We owe our existence to those who answered duty's call over and over again. From Trenton to Normandy, from Yorktown to Iwo Jima, we have been defended and defined by those who have served our country. It has been said that all gave some while some gave all. Today, however, there are many who think that they do not need to give at all. This attitude, in the long run, will serve the hedonist no better than it serves the nation which blesses him with abundant pleasures. National service is a national obligation and a personal responsibility owed by one and by all.

Accordingly, the United States should adopt a system of national service by all its citizens. With the exception of individuals who exist in a virtually vegetative state and are simply incapable of rendering any service, there will be no exemptions. This service would begin upon the completion of high school, or upon dropping out from high school and as soon as the individual has reached the age of seventeen. The period of service will be for at least two years. All inductees will undergo the same basic training that will include physical fitness, elementary military and survival training, and instruction in ethics and morals. Upon conclusion of this basic training (estimated to be approximately four months), the inductees will then go on to specialized training in either military or civilian forms of national service. Both civilian and military forms of service will be acceptable, although military service will be given preferential considerations which could include higher pay, a shorter period of service (though nothing shorter than two years will be granted – civilian service could be greater than twenty-four months), or a greater severance payment. Those who choose the military option will go on to receive advanced training and will be incorporated into our armed forces as would any basic inductee today. Those who choose the civilian option will also receive specialized training for the area of service where they are needed. Congress will designate the various service options where these civilian national servants will work. A substantial portion of the civilian national servants will also be available to serve at approved state and local activities. Living conditions will be Spartan and periodic pay will be meager. Again, this is national service, not a paid vacation. States and communities which employ some of these national servants will be expected to contribute to their pay and compensation; but all civilian pay and compensation will be equal, regardless of whether the service is provided to a national, state, or local agency. Upon completion of one's period of service, he or she will receive a severance payment which can be used to help finance a college education or begin one's career.

A variation on this form of service may be granted to those who choose to pursue a medical career (medical technicians, nurses, pharmacists, doctors, etc.) or a legal career (paralegals, lawyers, etc). These individuals will be allowed to complete their professional education. After this they will be required to perform their national service in full. Upon completion of their basic training, they will be assigned to serve where their skills can be put to good use.

After the Nazi invasion of Poland in September of 1939, the federal government authorized the development of a lightweight vehicle that could transport men and equipment in on- and off-road conditions. Ford Motor's contribution to the war-effort was a quarter-ton specialized truck designated "GP" for "general purpose." "GP" soon got shortened to "Jeep", and the rest, as they say, is history. The above proposal for universal national service would also be an excellent general purpose vehicle for accomplishing a variety of worthwhile objectives.

It would insure that we always had an adequate number of qualified individuals for our armed forces. Recruiters could be given more productive labors.

It would provide an army of qualified national servants who were ready to:

> * Assist various public works activities (road repairs, public safety jobs, public security aids, low-skill tasks at government agencies and buildings, etc.)
> * Assist various humanitarian activities around the nation (help out at food missions for the needy, retrain the chronically unemployed for productive lives, provide low-skill labor for hospitals and clinics, serve as childcare providers for low-income workers, etc.)

* Be available for mobilization in case of national or local emergencies (earthquakes, floods, fires, storm damage, terrorist attacks, etc.)

The medical and legal professionals who deferred their training could provide useful services both to civilian and military government agencies. They also could be used to provide low-cost legal and medical services to the indigent.

This program would ultimately result in a trained, national reserve force that could be mobilized in case of war or national emergency.

Beyond these obvious benefits, there are many other not-so-obvious blessings that would accrue. Ill-advised policies and programs over the last several decades have contributed to the decay of our moral fiber in America. (More on that later.) In short, tens of millions of Americans were never taught how to behave properly by their parents or their schools. As a result, their dysfunctional conduct causes a wide range of personal and social problems. Any hope for reversing and correcting this condition would likely take a generation or two with the tools currently available to us. However, universal national service could be a very powerful device for effecting meaningful reform and in a fraction of that time. Most of us who have undertaken basic military training have seen this. Individuals who exhibit unproductive and anti-social conduct are quickly "reprogrammed" and often turned into productive team-players – and in a remarkably short period of time. And for all the "usual suspects" among the Deceivers and charlatans who like to whine about military training quashing individuality, I simply say, "Look around." Most of the brightest shining examples of American ingenuity and individualism have a military background. Good military training does not quash individuality – it hones it.

The national servant's training would teach and inculcate such values as morality, personal and collective responsibility, compassion, team spirit, honor, respect for others and their property, and a strong work ethic. Given the average age of the inductees, we would be in a superb position to lessen drug and alcohol abuse by countering the budding behaviors and severing the associations which lead to them. Similarly, we would have an excellent opportunity to (1) break the bonds that may have already led to gang membership, (2) teach a more honorable and productive lifestyle, and (3) provide alternatives to returning to a gang once a national servant's duty is completed. All of this could have an immense impact on individual and social conduct. It would engender benefits that would range from greater productivity to reduced crime to more civility in general.

Again, the "usual suspects" among the Deceivers and charlatans can be expected to sound the alarm about "value coercion" and "brainwashing." Nonsense! All societies teach values. There would be no commonality of identity and purpose if they did not. Furthermore, there is nothing in the values that this program would instill that could be questioned or objected to by any reasonable person. We do not propose to force a religion upon anyone; we merely seek to promote those mores and manners which make for a successful and genteel society. As for "brainwashing" – "mouth-washing" perhaps as we work to create a more respectful American – but "brainwashing" is simply an ideological epithet used by the very people who are trying to accomplish what they are protesting. I served for many years and with many people in the armed forces of the United States. The number of individuals whom I can recall who were "brainwashed" by this experience can be counted on the fingers of no hands – in other words, none. Some people who came in nuts left nuts; but I know of no one who was made nuts by the values that were taught.

In summary, universal national service would solve a variety of problems and would provide even more blessings to the individual and the nation at large. It would be eminently fair and very effective. What is more, *every* American would be able to stand a little taller knowing that he or she had contributed to making the United States the greatest nation in history, and *every* American would have a greater vested interest in keeping it that way.

PART THREE

A MORAL AMERICA

CHAPTER ELEVEN

THE "X" FACTOR

In 1831, a young French historian and political thinker named Alexis de Tocqueville arrived in the United States with his friend, Gustave de Beaumont. They stayed for nine months. Their expressed purpose was to study this new land and, hopefully, to gain a better understanding of the sources of its strength and uniqueness. De Tocqueville then wrote down his observations in a two-volume work that would come to be known as *Democracy in America*, first published in 1835 and 1840. It is interesting and revealing to take note of de Tocqueville's first impression of America.

"Upon my arrival in the United States, the religious aspect of the country was the first thing that struck my attention; and the longer I stayed there, the more did I perceive the great political consequences resulting from this state of things, to which I was unaccustomed. In France I had almost always seen the spirit of religion and the spirit of freedom pursuing courses diametrically opposed to each other; but in America I found that they were intimately united, and that they reigned in common over the same country."

De Tocqueville correctly observed that our Christian heritage and beliefs were inextricably woven into the fabric of America. In fact, one could not understand the uniqueness and greatness of the United States apart from its Christianity. De Tocqueville is attributed with having penned a passage that is remarkable both for the clarity of its insight as well as the power of its prediction. "America is great because America is good, and if America ever ceases to be good, America will cease to be great." There has been some debate as to whether de Tocqueville ever really wrote this line. Regardless of how that debate turns out, two things are abundantly clear: (1) the remark is consistent with de Tocqueville's observations and conclusions and (2) the remark is very true, irrespective of who wrote it. The greatness of America has walked hand-in-hand with its goodness. In fact, this journey has not been side-by-side but rather in trace, for our greatness has followed our goodness. Sadly, tragically, that has been changing. We have taken a different path from that of goodness for many years now; and, as predicted, our greatness has waned. This is no idle coincidence. It is a rock-hard inevitability.

Over the last several decades commentators have utilized newspapers, magazines, radio, and television to focus our attention on the abundant evidence of America's decline. Various pundits have offered their

analyses of and solutions for this decay. The most prominent of these have concentrated on the political or economic or sociologic roots of our deteriorating condition.
What has been substantially omitted from this discussion, however, is the fact that if we fail to rebuild a "good"
America, nothing else will matter. Regardless of how
brilliant any plan for political or economic or sociologic
reconstruction may be, if that construction is erected
upon a rotten moral foundation, the edifice is doomed
to collapse.

As was written earlier, the proponents of big government and little liberty don't have a clue about how to heal
this land. More and more Americans are starting to realize this as we suffer from the effects of big government
and big deficits. Many are rediscovering the virtues of
big liberty and limited government which characterized
the glory years of American growth and prosperity. They
boisterously clamor for greater individual freedom and
for cutting back the size and scope of government. That is
good as far as it goes, but it doesn't go far enough. There
is another factor – the "X" factor – without which greater
freedom and limited government are not only unattain-
able, they are downright dangerous and ultimately suicidal. The "X" factor – the essential precondition without
which greater freedom and limited government are destined to fail – is morality.

We could go into a protracted philosophical discussion of this, but let's not. Two simple questions will
illustrate the truth of this statement. First, what do you

think would happen if we gave a great deal of personal freedom to an immoral people? The answer is obvious. They will do immoral things, and the nation will quickly degenerate into what I call a "penitentiary society" – a nation populated by criminals but without the benefit of the bars and guards to restrain them. Who would want to live in such a hedonistic Hades? The only winners would be the most vicious and exploitative among us. Second, what do you think would happen if we set up a limited, relatively weak government to administer over such an immoral people? Again, the answer is obvious. We would experience chaos, havoc, anarchy, and eventually despotism because the people will not long tolerate the degree of profound insecurity which would result. They would quickly sell out to the first strong man who promised them safety.

The annals of History are replete with proof of this proposition, but let me offer just one. John Adams – superstar of the American Revolution, first Vice President of the United States, second President of the United States, and a devout Christian – predicted the failure of the French Revolution when our own revolution had succeeded only a few years before. Why? Because theirs took place in a society with loose or no morals, as Adams had seen for himself when he served as an ambassador to France during the War for Independence. And just as predicted, the French Revolution quickly devolved into the Reign of Terror and the despotic imperial administration of Napoleon.

The Tree of Liberty cannot survive, much less thrive, in just any kind of soil. It needs the nutrients provided by a moral society or it will wither and perish. The Founders understood this very well, but it was perhaps best expressed by someone who studied them. Robert Winthrop was Speaker of the U.S. House of Representatives for the thirtieth Congress in the 1840's. He once said, "Men, in a word, must necessarily be controlled either by a power within them or by a power without them; either by the Word of God or by the strong arm of man; either by the Bible or by the bayonet."

If the "inner policeman" fails, the outer policeman will gladly step in to reestablish order – often brutally. When a nation lacks a moral populace, the only way to restrain evil and prevent social disintegration is through the power of some autocratic social institution, like the state. It therefore follows, ***if you love liberty, then you must preach and achieve morality.*** It is so important that we acknowledge and learn the lesson from those last eleven words that I will repeat them. ***If you love liberty, then you <u>must</u> preach and achieve morality.***

Morality is absolutely indispensable to the survival and success of a free society; and a free society is absolutely indispensable for a prosperous nation and a life worth living. True morality bestows upon a society some remarkable and indispensable blessings – blessings which nurture and nourish that society. In the first place, it provides a code of conduct that encourages each individual to pursue a loftier ambition and a greater good

105

than mere self-interest. True morality preaches that there is something better than "I" – that there is a higher goal and a better way. And yet, strangely, we find that when we sacrifice our personal interests for the sake of that greater good, we often end up being personally blessed in ways that are far superior to anything that the path of blind self-interest can ever attain.

True morality offers other blessings to the nation wise enough to embrace it. True morality provides the glue that holds a society together and the polar star that guides it. Without this glue, societies crumble. Without this guiding star, nations wander aimlessly. Now think about it. Isn't this exactly what has been going on in the United States for a great many years?

What is an "American"? We don't have "Americans" anymore. We have Afro-Americans, Hispanic-Americans, Asian-Americans, Euro-Americans, Native-Americans – and each one puts more emphasis on the adjective which precedes the word "American" than on the word "American" itself.

And what does it mean to be "American" anymore? Think about it. What do we stand for?

I was born a few years after the conclusion of World War II, and the memory of that war – what we did and why – was still very much alive in the American culture. My dad fought in that war. He had been a B-24 pilot. He was shot up several times before he was finally shot down on his eighteenth mission; and I was so proud of him for bombing the dog-snot out of those Nazi monsters. Even as a little kid only about five or six years old, I knew what it meant to be an American. Oh, my notion wasn't very sophisticated or very detailed, but I knew two things about my country: first, the United States did what was right; and, second, the United States didn't lose. Like I said, it wasn't very sophisticated, but by golly, if that's all you can say about your country, well, I think you've said just about enough. Now, let me ask you this: Can we still say that about our country – that the United States does what is right and that the United States never loses? Something terrible has happened to our country.

Morality – true morality – is indispensable to the survival and success of a great and free nation. But what is true morality, and where does it come from?

The first thing we need to know about true morality is that it is not man-made. Humans give us philosophy. Only God can create morality. Humans give us opinions. God gives us truth. The works of humans are ephemeral and fleeting. The works of God are unchanging and eternal.

Now, I know it has been said that what God giveth, God can taketh away, but He never changes what is right and what is wrong. That is not the case with men. What man giveth, man can – and probably will – taketh away – even concepts of right and wrong. You see, the problem with secular, humanist, man-made concepts of morality is that they are conditional, relativistic – which means, you can't count on them. They change – often unpredictably. They can be one thing yesterday, a different thing today, and yet something else tomorrow. It can be one thing for me and another for you. How can you build on such an unstable foundation? You cannot. But that is not the case with true morality. True morality is the same yesterday, today, and tomorrow; and true morality is the same for one and all. True morality doesn't change. It is universal. It is eternal. It is from God and God alone. And if a nation is to be blessed by true morality, then that nation must be founded upon, rooted in, and springing up from "the laws of nature and of nature's God…." "God", that sounds familiar. I know I've heard that somewhere before. Oh yeah, it is from the Declaration of Independence – the founding document of the United States of America. This country was founded upon, it was rooted in, and it did spring up from true morality. Furthermore, the Founders were quite clear about their understanding of the source of true morality: it was from what they frequently called "true religion" which they unashamedly and unequivocally pronounced to be Christianity. Don't take my word for it. Listen to them.

John Adams – "Our Constitution was made only for a moral and religious people. It is wholly inadequate to the government of any other."

Charles Carroll, signer of the Declaration of Independence – "[W]ithout morals a republic cannot subsist any length of time; they therefore who are decrying the Christian religion, whose morality is so sublime and pure… are undermining the *solid foundation of morals, the best security for the duration of free governments."*

Noah Webster -- *"[T]he Christian religion, in its purity, is the basis, or rather the source of all genuine freedom in government… and I am persuaded that no civil government of a republican form can exist and be durable in which the principles of that religion have not a controlling influence."*

John Jay, *first Chief Justice of the United States Supreme Court – it is "the duty of all wise, free, and virtuous governments to countenance and encourage virtue and religion."*

Oliver Ellsworth, *third Chief Justice of the United States Supreme Court – "The legislature, charged with the great interests of the community, may, and ought to countenance, aid, and protect religious institutions… the legislature may aid the maintenance of [Christianity], whose benign influence on morals is universally acknowledged. It may be added that this principle has been long recognized, and is too intimately connected with the peace, order, and happiness of the state to be abandoned."*

William Paterson, *signer of the Constitution and United States Supreme Court Justice – "Religion and morality… [are] necessary to good government, good order, and good laws."*

Joseph Story, *founder of the Harvard School of Law and United States Supreme Court Justice – "Indeed, the right of a society or government to [participate] in matters of religion will hardly be contested by any persons who believe that piety, religion, and morality are intimately connected with the well being of the state and indispensable to the* *administration of civil justice…. It is, indeed, difficult to conceive how any civilized society can well exist without them. And, at all events, it is impossible for those who believe in the truth of Christianity as a Divine revelation to doubt that it is the especial duty of government to foster and encourage it among all the citizens and subjects…."*

Patrick Henry – *"It cannot be emphasized too clearly and too often that this nation was founded, not by religionists, but by Christians; not on religion, but on the Gospel of Jesus Christ."*

The list of statements by our Founders attesting to the Christian nature of the United States goes on seemingly endlessly, but I would be horribly remiss if I did not include this one more. **Hear it**. *"… it is the duty of all Nations to acknowledge the providence of Almighty God, to obey his will, to be grateful for his benefits, and humbly to implore his protection and favor…."* – George Washington, who was not only the first President of the United States but also the President of the Constitutional Convention. The very man who presided over our Constitution's creation proclaimed that "it is the duty of all Nations to acknowledge the providence of Almighty God [and] to obey his will…." Does this surprise us? Why should we think that Washington would do anything else? The Constitution's overseer was merely faithfully repeating and institutionalizing the sentiment expressed in the Declaration of Independence: "We hold these truths to be self-evident, that all men are created equal, that they are endowed by their Creator with certain unalienable Rights, that among these are Life, Liberty, and the pursuit of Happiness. That to secure these rights, Governments are instituted among Men…." In case you missed the supreme importance of what was just declared, read it backwards: Governments are instituted among men to secure the rights that were given to them by their Creator. In other words, ***governments exist to do the will of God!*** The Founders never intended a separation of religion and state. They sought a marriage of God and government.

The Founders understood what we have shied away from, if not outright abandoned: You cannot have a free society and a limited government without true morality. True morality comes from true religion, and true religion is Christianity. It therefore follows that you cannot have a free society and a limited government without Christianity.

If you love liberty, then you must preach and achieve Christianity!

And what can we expect if we should be so foolish as to continue on this wayward, secular path – if we should choose to ignore this truth which the Founders understood so well? Noah Webster perceived the ultimate outcome with a chilling clarity. He wrote, "[I]f we and our posterity reject religious instruction and authority, violate the rules of eternal justice, trifle with the injunctions of morality, and recklessly destroy the political constitution which holds us together, no man can tell how sudden a catastrophe may overwhelm us that shall bury all our glory in profound obscurity." In other words, America is great because America is good, and if America ever ceases to be good, America will cease to be great. It may even cease to be.

We *have* to put God back in government, and that means that we *have* to put religion back in politics. Let us now consider a few moral issues which simply *must* be addressed.

CHAPTER TWELVE

ATROCITIES

Pol Pot was the leader of the Khmer Rouge in Cambodia. He described his objective as "building social-ism." He killed nearly two million of his countrymen in order to accomplish this. He is considered to be a mon-ster. Adolf Hitler was the leader of the National Socialist German Workers' Party – Nazis. He killed approximately ten million in his concentration camps – six million of those being Jews – because they didn't fit into his plans for an Aryan, socialist world order. He is considered to be a monster. Joseph Stalin was the leader of the Union of Soviet Socialist Republics. It is estimated that he had about twenty million people executed in his Gulags (prison camps) and purges because they impeded his march toward the Communist ideal. He is considered to be a monster. Mao Zedong was the leader of the People's Republic of China. Estimates of the number of citizens he had slaughtered in order to achieve his socialist uto-pia range from a low of over twenty million to nearly fifty million. He is considered to be a monster. In less than forty years since the passage of Roe v. Wade, even more innocent Americans have been put to death by the practice of abortion than were killed by the mega-monster, Mao Zedong. What word should we use to describe those who have perpetrated this atrocity?

In all the wars that the United States has fought – from the Revolution to Afghanistan – approximately 910,000 Americans have died. In the thirty-eight years since the Supreme Court legalized abortion, it is estimated that approximately fifty-three million Americans have died – in their mother's womb. What this means is that the secular, progressive liberals are responsible for more than fifty-eight times as many dead Americans as all the monarchs, tyrants, and terrorists we have ever confronted combined. We lose more Americans *a day* to abortion than were lost in all the terrorist attacks on September 11, 2001. And while hundreds of thousands gathered in Washington, D.C. to protest this atrocity, President Obama celebrated, "Roe v. Wade, the Supreme Court decision that protects women's health and reproductive freedom, and affirms a fundamental principle: that government should not intrude on private family matters…. And on this anniversary, I hope that we will recommit ourselves more broadly to ensuring that our daughters have the same rights, the same freedoms, and the same opportunities as our sons to fulfill their dreams." Mr. President, it's pretty hard for anyone – son or daughter – to pursue any dream from within a plastic bag labeled "Biologic Waste."

God does not make trash, and this genocide must stop!

Few things demonstrate the moral abasement of America more than the practice of abortion where our most innocent and helpless brothers and sisters are executed simply because their existence is inconvenient. Pol Pot, Hitler, Stalin, and Mao could at least claim that their massacres were perpetrated in order to achieve the future blessing of an ideal society. They were horribly wrong about both their goals and their methods, but how do we compare this with those whose only justification for mass murder is that little Jane or Johnny simply got in the way?

"Reproductive freedom" did I hear you say, Mr. President? My apologies, sir. I guess I missed that one when I read the Declaration and the Constitution and the Bible. I thought we were supposed to respect life. That's the point, isn't it? You either respect life or you don't; and when you don't, it opens the door for all manner of atrocities.

It is said that politics makes strange bedfellows. Strange bedfellows, yes – and perverse lines of thinking as well. Over a century-and-a-half ago we fought a Civil War to preserve the Union and end slavery, among other things. Today, we are pretty much all in agreement that it is terribly wrong to deny people their freedom and to treat them like property simply because of their race. Well, if this is so, then how much worse is it to deny people their lives and dispose of them like garbage simply

because of their age? Ironically, the same political ele-
ments (leftists and their fellow travelers) that are most
likely to resurrect the ghosts of slavery are also the ones
most likely to ignore the voices of the ghosts of abortion.
Hypocrisy!

Hypocrites, yes; but they are clever about it. They
wrap themselves in the flag (which must chafe more than
a little for them) and then ring the "Liberty Bell." They use
a tactic against which many Americans cannot conceive
a defense: rights. Our nation's claim to independence
was founded upon the idea that God-given rights war-
ranted our rebellion against Great Britain. America is all
about rights, and anyone who can claim that they have a
"right" to a particular thing has adopted a powerful and
proven tactic that is likely to succeed; and this is precisely
how the proponents of abortion try to justify their cause.
They claim that a woman has the "right" to do whatever
she wishes with her own body. Really? Does that extend
to me, too? Am I allowed to take parts of my body, wrap
them around a baseball bat and try to beat some sense
into you? Of course not! Liberties and rights are not
unrestricted, and no responsible theory about liberties
and rights has ever contended that they are. And one
of the most universally acknowledged restrictions on liberties is that personal behavior may be regulated when
it begins to impact on another. The old saying is that
the freedom of my fist ends just short of the tip of your
nose. A woman is pretty much free to do what she wants
with her empty womb, but the moment that womb is

occupied by another life that freedom ends. The "rights" of another must be taken into account; and since that other is in no position to do this for him or herself, society must step in where individual conscience fails. Except in instances where the life of the mother is in indisputable jeopardy, abortion cannot be justified – and this circumstance of extreme jeopardy is a condition which many doctors themselves admit is extremely rare.

Abortion must end. How? Legislate it out of existence. "Oh, but we tried that", you protest. "The courts overruled us." Yes, they did. Thomas Jefferson anticipated this. Of the three branches of government, he feared the greatest danger to the original intent of the Constitution lay in the hands of the very people who were entrusted with the responsibility of protecting it: the courts. "The Constitution", he said, "is a mere thing of wax in the hands of the judiciary which they may twist and shape into any form they please." He feared that the Constitution would become like wax in the hands of an activist court, and so it has. Modern courts have twisted and perverted the original intent of the Constitution to the point where many decisions bear no resemblance to the ideals established by the Founders. The Constitution has become like wax in the hands of crusading justices, but it is only as malleable as we allow it to be. The time has come for we the people to stand for the document which guided us to glory and to stand against those who would trample it for the sake of personal ideology. How do we do that?

Supreme Court justices take the same oath of office to "preserve, protect and defend the Constitution of the United States" that the President does. When it becomes apparent that they have failed to do this, we must demand that they be impeached. They have violated the most basic and critical of civil trusts, and they deserve not only removal from the bench, but imprisonment as well. Up until now they had nothing to fear, other than some whining from politicians, commentators, and various interest groups. I suspect that as soon as our justices realize that they will be held personally accountable to a righteously indignant populace for their official misconduct, they will start to be a little more careful about their rulings. The justices' apologists, no doubt, will argue that this proposal threatens the independence of the judiciary. Is the President free to do whatever he wants with no consequence? Are the members of Congress free to do whatever they want with no consequence? Of course not. They are accountable for their errant behavior, and so must be the justices. It is important to defend the independence of each branch of government, but not to the extent that this independence jeopardizes the very principles which they are charged to protect and defend. The judiciary deserves no greater protection from their errors than do the members of Congress or the President.

Abortion is an abomination to everything which we hold dear – from the ideals of our Christian faith to the bedrock principles of defending the rights of life, liberty, and the pursuit of happiness. Those rights apply to the unborn as well, and it is long past the time for us to give a voice to those who cannot speak for themselves.

In writing of the atrocity of slavery, Thomas Jefferson lamented, "I tremble for my country when I reflect that God is just; that his justice cannot sleep forever." If we have reason to tremble because we have treated the Father's children like property, how much more need we fear because we have treated them like trash?

CHAPTER THIRTEEN

ABOMINATIONS

Undermine the morality of America and you undermine America itself. Destroy our moral fiber, and you destroy us. It is tragic and deplorable that our enemies have understood this far better than our defenders have. Over half a century ago a book was written by a former FBI Special Agent and Chief of Police for Salt Lake City, W. Cleon Skousen. It was entitled, *The Naked Communist*. Skousen's investigations had unearthed many not-so-secret plans for destroying a free America and replacing it with a socialist regime, and ultimately a Communist society. He spelled out forty-five specific goals for accomplishing this without firing a shot. Goals 24 through 28 as well as 40 and 41 illustrate how clearly our enemies perceive the need to destroy our moral foundations. They read as follows:

#24. Eliminate all laws governing obscenity by calling them "censorship" and a violation of free speech and free press.

#25. Break down cultural standards of morality by promoting pornography and obscenity in books, magazines, motion pictures, radio and TV.

#26. Present homo-sexuality, degeneracy and promiscuity as "Normal, natural, healthy."

#27. Infiltrate the churches and replace revealed religion with "social" religion. Discredit the Bible and emphasize the need for intellectual maturity which does not need a "religious crutch."

#28. Eliminate prayer or any phase of religious expression in the schools on the ground that it violates the principle of "separation of church and state."

#40. Discredit the family as an institution. Encourage promiscuity and easy divorce.

#41. Emphasize the need to raise children away from the negative influence of parents. Attribute prejudices, mental blocks and retarding of children to suppressive influence of parents." [Skousen, W. Cleon, *The Naked Communist*. Ensign Publishing Company. © 1958. Pages 260-262.]

Undoubtedly, Skousen was disparaged and discredited in his day as some kind of kooky, conspiratorial theorist who spent his weekends looking under moldy rocks for Communists. Today, over fifty years later, we can see that every one of these goals has been pursued and with the desired effects. The decline of America the Great has proceeded in lockstep with the decay of America the Good. If we want to stop the decline, then we must stop the decay.

A deep and abiding respect for freedom has always been an important quality in the identity of America. But "freedom" is not the same as "licentiousness", and it is licentiousness which has characterized America's hedonistic behavior over the last several decades. "Licentiousness" is unprincipled freedom. It disregards accepted rules, mores, and conventions. As such, it inevitably constitutes a profound threat to traditional society because it does not respect its rules and manners. Historically, Americans have been endowed with a great deal of freedom because it was understood that they would know better than to abuse it. Our strong moral code, rooted in our Judeo-Christian values, prompted the "internal policeman" to regulate our behavior before the external policeman had to. We could be free because we could be trusted. That is no longer the case. The Deceivers and charlatans have exploited our commitment to liberty by urging us to take these liberties to absurd extremes. The ultimate result, whether intended or not, will be to destroy them altogether. We must not allow this to happen. It may seem paradoxical, but the best way to preserve our freedoms is to voluntarily limit the most extreme and pernicious manifestations of them ourselves. But then, is this really so paradoxical? Think about it. Responsible parents grant their children more and more freedom **only so long as they demonstrate that they will not abuse this trust.** When the children show that they cannot be trusted, their freedoms are cut back or eliminated altogether.

Societies work the same way. They have to or they will collapse.

We mentioned in the last chapter that all responsible theories of liberty have acknowledged the need to regulate that liberty in order to guard against harmful abuses. Liberty is never absolute, except in the jungle, and then it usually only applies to the alpha male. All others are either slaves or corpses. We must reassert our right as a nation to regulate and prohibit those extreme abuses of freedom which undermine our national well-being. This is not at all unprecedented nor unconstitutional. Back in the nineteenth century a Supreme Court case ruled that the Mormon practice of polygamy could be outlawed. Religious freedom notwithstanding, this was going too far. In the twentieth century a Supreme Court Justice said that yelling "Fire!" in a crowded theater when there was no fire was not permissible. Freedom of speech notwithstanding, this was going too far. By the same token, we must assert our justification to outlaw other destructive forms of behavior – like pornography and public obscenity – as going too far.

Similarly, we must defend against attacks on a moral America and on the institutions of the family and traditional marriage by forbidding homosexual "marriage." This is not an expression of homophobia; it is a defense of those Judeo-Christian values which undergird a moral American society. When the family fails, society falls.

Undoubtedly, my opponents will claim that this is an expression of some deep-seated hostility toward homosexuals. Hardly. I have homosexual family members. I have had homosexual friends. I have even gone way out of my way to help complete strangers who were homosexual simply because they needed it. I have a great deal of compassion for their condition, but I cannot condone the consummation of that condition. Is this because I am so wise as to know what is best for these individuals? No. It is because I believe that the Author of the Bible was that wise, and He condemned the behavior consistently from Old Testament to New. I remember a conversation I had on the matter with a friend who suggested that I was not showing true sympathy for these people. I returned the challenge and asked him if he fully appreciated the cost of his "sympathy." I asked, "How many hundreds of thousands or even millions of homosexuals would still be alive today, would still be healthy today, would still be with their friends and loved ones today, would still be leading productive, meaningful lives today if they only would have observed the Biblical prohibitions against homosexual behavior?" God knew the consequence of "acting out." He was trying to protect His children, not spoil their fun.

Perhaps the greatest failure which moral America has committed in fighting against the rising tide to legalize homosexual marriage is that we have allowed its proponents to get away with calling it a "right." As we said before, America was founded upon the idea that there are God-given rights and that they must be defended. As soon as one side allows the other side to claim the existence of a right, well, you're already behind in the count 0 and 2 with a blazing hot fastball coming in high and tight. Before we talk about "Biblical" or "traditional" values – which the opposition doesn't respect anyway – we must challenge the "right" to homosexual marriage the moment it falls out of someone's mouth.

"Rights" are not "wannas." You do not have the right to do anything you "wanna" do. "Rights" are special, fundamental liberties that usually find their authority and justification in one of three places: (1) a generally recognized "Higher Authority", like God as revealed in holy Scripture, (2) a generally recognized fundamental legal document, like the Declaration of Independence or the Constitution, or (3) a generally recognized common practice which is held to be integral to the lives of the people, like common law. Can the claim of a "right" to homosexual marriage be based on any one of these? No.

First let us look at common practice or common law. It was not that long ago that homosexuals chose to remain "in the closet" because their behavior was so detestable to so many people that the homosexual feared vilification, persecution, and even lynching. I certainly do not condone such reactions, but they demonstrate how commonplace and vehement were the feelings against homosexual conduct. In fact, in many states, what the homosexual called "love" the state called a crime. There is no basis for a claim to "right" status in common law.

Next, what about God? Here, again, no dice. The Old Testament, the New Testament, and even the Koran condemn homosexual behavior in the strongest terms – terms like "abhorrent", "detestable", and "abomination."

Is there any hope to base a claim to "right" status in either the Constitution or the Declaration of Independence? Certainly not in the Constitution. In fact, given the devout Christian faith of most of the drafters of the Constitution, we can only suspect that had they anticipated modern trends they would have specifically forbidden such a threat to their beloved, moral America. Some campaigners for homosexual marriage might try to pin their hopes on the Declaration's glowing defense of "life, liberty, and the pursuit of happiness." Homosexuals, they may argue, are only seeking the liberty to pursue their happiness. Nice try, but anything more than a purely superficial glance will reveal that this notion won't fly. As we have stated before, not any liberty is permissible, nor is any pursuit of happiness. After all, drug dealers, robbers, and rapists are merely trying to pursue their happiness. Once we look at this famous remark of the Declaration in context, we quickly realize that there is no defense for homosexual marriage. Remember, the rights with which we are endowed came from the Creator – you know, the same God who condemned homosexual behavior as an abomination. I don't think that this can be claimed as one of the pursuits of happiness that He would approve.

Strike three. You're out! Pornography, public obscenity, and homosexual marriage – as well as other abuses – all fall within the scope of "regulatable behavior" due to their licentious and pernicious impact.

Any defense of America which does not include a stalwart defense of moral America will not stand. This is not some philosophical abstraction. Look throughout history; look around the world today. Where do you ever see freedom and prosperity coexist for any length of time where there is no morality? You don't. The America of our dreams is the America of our past. That was a moral America. That was a Christian America. If you love liberty – if you want to rebuild America the Great – then you must preach and achieve America the Good.

CHAPTER FOURTEEN

OPERATION REDEMPTION

Whatever principles and values are taught to the current generation of students will inspire and guide the next generation of teachers, which includes schoolmasters, parents, and politicians alike. Samuel Adams rightly observed that "Neither the wisest constitution nor the wisest laws will secure the liberty and happiness of a people whose manners are universally corrupt." Accordingly, he urged that "ministers and philosophers, statesmen and patriots unite their endeavors to renovate the age by educating their little boys and girls and leading them in the study and practice of the exalted virtues of the Christian system." Both our greatest patriots and our vilest enemies agree on this point. The inculcation of morals is vital to the preservation and prosperity of our free society. Our patriots have worked diligently to establish and perpetuate an educational system that teaches such morals. Our enemies have worked even more diligently to destroy it. Recall Communist goals Number 26 and 28 from the previous chapter. Number 26: Present homo-sexuality, degeneracy and promiscuity as "normal, natural, healthy." Precisely this is being incorporated into textbooks and curricula in many states – even at the elementary level. Number 28: Eliminate prayer or any phase of religious expression in the schools on the ground that it violates the principle of "separation of church and state." This goal has not only been attempted, it has been firmly established in our public schools.

Many bemoan the decline of public education in America over the last several decades. Pundits have pointed the finger at various causes, but few have alleged a connection between this decline and the divestiture of moral training from our educational process. There is much that we need to do to reform public education in America. We must decentralize this process and virtually eliminate any federal influence in that process. We didn't use to have federal control, and we came out smelling like roses. We've got it now and we stink to high heaven. I submit that this is not an idle coincidence. We need to return the emphasis to helping the children – not on plumping the pay and benefits packages for the teachers and administrators. We need to reestablish discipline and insist on good behavior and good performance. We need to acknowledge that teaching everybody in his or her native language (assuming that this language is not English) only hurts the child's ability to succeed later in life in America and encourages a fractured society instead of a united one. We've got to worry less about promoting "self-esteem" and worry more about promoting self-worth. We've got to stop teaching the test and start teaching what will stand the test of time. But if we truly wish "to renovate the age", then we must resume teaching the moral values which served us so well for so long and which constitute the only way to rebuild a free society worthy of our faith and devotion. How do we do this? I propose a nation-wide campaign called **Operation Redemption**. The particulars are as follows:

1. <u>MISSION.</u> Our mission is to rebuild the United States of America spiritually, politically, and economically according to Biblical principles and the ideals of our Founders. An important way in which we can achieve this objective will be by reforming the public schools in the local communities.

2. <u>EXECUTION.</u> The Christian and patriotic community will work together to:

    a. Select qualified and committed Christians to run for local school boards.

    b. Assist these individuals in running for, and being elected to, their local school boards.

    c. Provide a carefully prepared portfolio of resolutions to be introduced, passed, and implemented by these school boards. These resolutions will re-establish Bible-based moral teachings, lessons on the Ten Commandments, and voluntary, non-denominational prayer. These resolutions will seek to faithfully return the type of Biblical and moral training that characterized public school education in the United States from our inception through the middle of the twentieth century – the glory years of America.

d. Provide advice and training to these school board members on how to deal with the criticism that we anticipate these resolutions will engender.

e. Provide legal assistance to deal with the anticipated opposition. This assistance will include a defense team to aid where court action results.

f. Provide advice and assistance to these Christian board members so they can be re-elected in the future thereby securing our accomplishments and continuing our momentum for reform.

3. <u>ANTICIPATED COMMUNITY REACTION.</u>

a. Many in the Christian community will support this course of action and its objectives. We count on these individuals and organizations to insure that our slate of Christian board members is elected, supported, and re-elected.

b. We can expect vehement opposition from others in the community who object to these policies. In many communities this opposition will be short-lived and will result in no formal legal challenge.

c. In other communities we can expect vehement opposition that will result in a formal legal challenge, quite probably with the assistance of the ACLU. This is exactly what we want. Our ultimate plan and desire is that a formal legal challenge and subsequent appeals will result in the matter being reconsidered by the United States Supreme Court resulting in a reversal of various Court rulings made in recent decades.

4. <u>RATIONALE FOR THIS COURSE OF ACTION.</u>

Traditionally, school board elections are poorly attended. Accordingly, it should be easier and less costly to elect sympathetic candidates here than in other areas of government. In turn, this would allow us to begin to realize almost immediate results. We also believe that this is a weak point for the opposition and, therefore, a good place to attack. Beginning in 1947 with *Everson v. Board of Education*, the United States Supreme Court (and other lesser courts following the Supreme Court's lead) has fairly consistently worked to remove religion from the operations of public agencies, including our public schools. However, the "separation" language used in *Everson* and elsewhere is not faithful to the original language and intent of the Constitution and the First Amendment ("Congress shall make no law respecting an establishment of religion or **prohibiting** the free exercise thereof...." emphasis added). These rulings have caused fundamental changes in public school policies and practices which are contrary to the long-established and successful traditions of American public school policies and practices – including policies and practices encouraged by drafters of the Constitution themselves. Furthermore, Supreme Court decisions have often been founded upon questionable rationales and practices. For example, in *Engel v. Vitale*, where the Court ruled to prohibit voluntary, nondenominational prayers at public school functions, the Court cited no precedents to justify their action. This is almost unheard of. Accordingly, we feel that we are in an excellent position to request and achieve a reversal of recent Supreme Court decisions which, themselves, were reversals of prevailing policies, practices, and judgments.

To couch this plan of action in military terms, we intend to strike at the enemy's weak spot. A determined and well-executed offensive can turn the tide and lead to ultimate victory.

It is also hoped that the publicity which is expected to surround this court battle will unify and inspire the Christian community to mobilize and work in a variety of other areas with the ultimate goal of taking back Christian America. The more the opposition fights us, the more determined we will become. So, if the opposition leaves us alone, we win. If they choose to fight us, we win big. The time has come to remember and trust Philippians 4:13, "I can do all things through Christ who strengthens me."

Resolved! In the Appendix at the back of this book I have included the text for a resolution to accomplish the goals described above. I hereby give permission to you to copy and use this resolution to pursue these goals. Go with God!

"Religion is the only solid basis of good morals; therefore education should teach the precepts of religion and the duties of man towards God." Gouverneur Morris, principal drafter and signer of the United States Constitution.

"Of all the dispositions and habits which lead to political prosperity, religion and morality are indispensable supports. In vain would that man claim the tribute of patriotism who should labor to subvert these great pillars of human happiness."
George Washington, President of the Constitutional Convention

PART FOUR

A CALL TO ACTION

CHAPTER FIFTEEN

INSEPARABLE

Some time ago I shared a few ideas for reforming America with a friend. He said that he liked them but then warned that, "We have a little problem." I am by no means clairvoyant, but I was pretty sure I knew what his "little problem" was. "What's that?", I asked. "Separation of Church and State", he answered. I smiled. "My friend, it's not as big a problem as you may think."

On occasion I have given a quiz to various groups of people. One of the questions is, "Where do we get the expression, 'separation of Church and State'?" It is a multiple choice question, and the answer options include the Declaration of Independence, the Constitution of the United States, and the First Amendment to the Constitution of the United States. There are other options as well, including the seemingly whimsical "a private letter written by Thomas Jefferson to a group of Baptists in Danbury, Connecticut." Guess what – the whimsical one wins. In 1947 the private words of comfort penned by a man who was not even in the country when the Constitution was written were elevated to the status of absolute criterion by which any matters pertaining to religion and government are decided. It seems that many of our justices have assumed unto themselves the power to rewrite the Constitution whenever it fails to give them the answer they want. As such, the justices are attacking the very document they are supposed to be defending. Apparently they presume a wisdom greater than that of the men who attended the Constitutional Convention back in 1787. I believe that arrogant presumption can and must be contested.

The Constitution specifically addresses religion in two places which detail three guiding principles. First, Article 6 states, "no religious test shall ever be required as a qualification to any office or public trust under the United States." In other words, we cannot require that a candidate for public office or public trust be a member of a certain religion, nor can we forbid anyone from holding a public office or trust because of their religion. Next, the First Amendment states, "Congress shall make no law respecting an establishment of religion, or prohibiting the free exercise thereof…." The so-called "Establishment Clause" was written to prevent the creation of an official state church. The "Free Exercise Clause" denies Congress the power to **prohibit** anyone from practicing his religion – within reason. There are some practices which are so objectionable to the norms of the general society that they have been deemed subject to regulation. For example, we already mentioned the practice of polygamy. Human sacrifices would also be on that list.

Now that we have refreshed our memory regarding what the Constitution requires, consider the following actions: saying a prayer at a school function; having an image of the Ten Commandments in a courthouse; installing a manger scene on public property at Christmastime; pledging allegiance to the flag including the words "under God"; engraving our currency with the national motto, "In God We Trust". Do any of these actions prevent anyone from holding a public office? Do any of them establish a state church or prohibit anyone from practicing his religion. **NO!** Accordingly, they all are clearly Constitutional, and yet each one of these activities has either been outlawed or at least seriously challenged by a court at some level in our country. How can this be? What is all the controversy about? It is about the real agenda of many on "the left" to undermine the moral underpinnings of America. The best way they have found to accomplish this is not with a frontal attack but by more devious and surreptitious means, namely, by relying on the rulings of their lackeys on the bench. First they rewrote Constitutional law by inserting the "separation of Church and State" principle into the mix; then they went even further by establishing another Constitutionally invisible standard – "endorsement." You see, the **real** Constitution didn't go far enough with the word "prohibit" to suit the desires of the Deceivers and charlatans. Having a plaque with the Ten Commandments in a courthouse does not "prohibit" anyone from practicing his religion (although it may point out to many who are there – especially those in orange jumpsuits – why they are there). The Deceivers, however, wanted the plaque gone, and so they had to substitute a new, more expansive word for "prohibit." The winner is "endorse." It now is commonplace to hear the Deceivers and their fellow travelers complain about an "unconstitutional **endorsement** of religion." The problem with that, of course, is that the words, "endorse" or "endorsement", are nowhere to be found or even hinted at in any of the portions of the Constitution dealing with religion. In fact, ***the Founders actually wanted to endorse religion, Christianity in particular.***

My, that sounds far-fetched in this day and age. Is there any support for such a wild claim? Absolutely.

The simple facts are these: (1) the Constitution of the United States is a Christian document, (2) the drafters of the Constitution never intended to remove God from government, and (3) many of the rulings of the Supreme Court concerning religion over the last sixty years are based upon the misguided opinions of a handful of justices and not upon a proper interpretation of the Constitution itself. Let's explore this a little further.

First, the Constitution is a Christian document. The Preamble of the Constitution explains just what this document is intended to do and just how it intends to do it. The purpose of the Constitution is "to form a more perfect Union, establish justice, insure domestic tranquility, provide for the common defense, promote the general welfare, and secure the blessings of liberty to ourselves and our posterity…." In order to accomplish these objectives, the people, through accepting this document, "do ordain and establish this Constitution for the United States of America."

Now, there was an interesting word – a strange word – used in the Preamble. Did you hear it? "Ordain." How often have you heard the word "ordain" used outside of a religious context? Oh, it can be. It means to properly set up or to establish, but the drafters already used the word "establish": we "do ordain **and establish** this Constitution…." The drafters were pretty particular. I don't think they would use the words "ordain" and "establish" if they intended them both to denote the same thing – as in, we "do establish and establish this Constitution." Well, if the authors of the Constitution did not intend the word "ordain" to mean "establish", the only other definition for ordain is religious in nature.

Just to make sure that I had this right, I looked up the word "ordain" in the 1828 edition of Noah Webster's *American Dictionary of the English Language*. Now why would I go to the trouble of looking up the word in this particular and rather ancient edition of the dictionary? Well, the *American Dictionary of the English Language* was the first **American** dictionary of the English language. Furthermore, it was composed by Noah Webster. Webster was a college student when the Declaration of Independence was drafted and approved. He was a soldier in the Revolutionary war and later served in the Connecticut General Assembly, the Massachusetts Legislature, and as a judge. He also influenced the drafting of portions of the United States Constitution, Article I, Section 8 in particular. What this all means is that Noah Webster would have had the same understanding of the word "ordain" as did the drafters of the Constitution. He was their contemporary. How did Webster define "ordain"? Well, he includes the secular reference to set up or to establish, but then he goes on with this: "to invest with a ministerial function or sacerdotal power; to introduce and establish or settle in the pastoral office with the customary forms and solemnities; as to ordain a minister of the gospel." He then makes a particular reference to this country. "In America, men are ordained over a particular church and congregation, or as evangelists without the charge of a particular church, or as deacons in the Episcopal church." And just in case you're a little shaky on the meaning of that word "sacerdotal", Webster defined it as "Pertaining to priests or the priesthood; priestly…."

The drafters of the Constitution deliberately included the word "ordain" when they commissioned this document to do its work. Someone or something that is ordained is authorized and charged to do the work of God. The Constitution is honoring and institutionalizing the principle established in the Declaration; namely, that governments are established to do the work of God. God is not hereby being separated from government. To the contrary, the government is being ordained to do His bidding.

Let's move on. Article I, Section 7, of the Constitution describes how laws are made. Once a bill has been passed by both the House of Representatives and the Senate, it goes to the President. If the President signs the bill, it becomes a law. The President may also veto a bill, but he only has a limited amount of time to act one way or the other. The Constitution says, "If any bill shall not be returned by the President within ten days (Sundays excepted) after it shall have been presented to him, the same shall be a law in like manner as if he had signed it…." So the President has ten days to act, not counting Sundays. **Not counting Sundays**? Gee, why do you suppose the authors of the Constitution chose **that** day to exclude? Oh, I don't know – maybe because it's the **Christian** Sabbath day, and you're not supposed to toil on the Sabbath, even if you are the President of the United States. For crying out loud, here's an example of the Blue Laws being written right into the Constitution of the United States! So much for keeping religion out of government. The Constitution, itself, institutionalizes a Biblical, Christian practice!

There are more evidences of the Christian nature of the Constitution, but my favorite little thorn with which to prick the sides and egos of the atheists, agnostics, and ACLU is found at the very end of the Constitution – about the place where everybody has stopped studying this grand document. Right at the conclusion of Article VII and right before the signatures comes this jewel. "DONE in convention by the unanimous consent of the states present the seventeenth day of September *in the Year of our Lord* one thousand seven hundred and eighty seven, and of the independence of the United States of America the Twelfth." (Emphasis added.) Gee, who do you suppose this "Lord" of ours is who lived one thousand seven hundred and eighty-seven years before? Is there any doubt? And please do not try to dismiss this as merely a manner of speech. The drafters of the Constitution were a contentious bunch. They argued over everything – even punctuation marks. There is no way they would have allowed this reference to "*our Lord*" to remain in the Constitution if they found any offense in it. In fact, there is another date, 1808, which is used twice in the Constitution, and in neither case does it include the phrase, "in the year of our Lord", which proves that the expression is not automatic but very deliberate.

So, let us summarize. The Constitution of the United States is "ordained" by the people to do the work of God, it recognizes uniquely Biblical and Christian practices, and it proclaims Jesus Christ to be our Lord. Far from separating itself from God, the Constitution embraces Him. And so too must today's America.

The first point I wished to make about the Constitution is that it is a *Christian* document. Enough said on this one. Let's move on to the second point, namely, that the drafters of the Constitution never intended to remove God from government. The evidence in support of this contention is so overwhelming that we should not even have to consider it – and we wouldn't have to if people only knew more about their own history. But since many – Supreme Court justices included – do not, let's take a brief look at this issue as well.

I think one of the best ways to resolve any dispute regarding what the authors of the Constitution may have intended in this area of religion is to see what those who understood the Constitution best actually did. In other words, did the drafters' actual behavior immediately after the enactment of the Constitution indicate that they wished God to be removed from government? Let's see.

The first Congress debated, drafted, and approved the First Amendment to the Constitution. This is the amendment that includes the famous "Establishment" and "Free Exercise" clauses regarding religion. Surely, these people would have had a clear understanding of what that amendment required and what it forbad. Well, one of the first orders of business undertaken by that very first Congress was to hire a chaplain – a Christian pastor – for each of the houses of Congress. He was to be paid with public funds and his job included the responsibility to offer a prayer at the convening of each house of Congress. In other words, government funds would be used to pay the salary of a Christian pastor to pray at government functions and in government facilities. Oh my. Please don't tell the Supreme Court justices about this. It would be so embarrassing for them to have to admit how ignorant and foolish they have been. Look, who do you think had a better understanding of the First Amendment – the very people who wrote it or nine political appointees some two hundred years after it was written? Let us continue.

On June 8, 1789, the initial draft of the First Amendment was offered by James Madison, later to become the 4th President of the United States and the man who is considered by many to be the "Father of the Constitution." That draft was subsequently debated and amended. During the course of that debate, Congressman Benjamin Huntington of Connecticut stated that he wanted to insure that "The amendment be made in such a way as to secure the rights of religion, but not to patronize those who professed no religion at all." Again, don't tell the Supreme Court.

On August 7, 1789, the Congress reenacted the Northwest Ordinance which had been previously enacted by the government under the Articles of Confederation – our first and less than successful constitution. Three days later President George Washington signed it into law. This is at the same time that the First Amendment is being formulated. The Northwest Ordinance states in Article III, "Religion, morality, and knowledge, being necessary to good government and the happiness of mankind, schools and the means of education shall forever be encouraged." Here we not only witness the government endorsing the spread of religion but also obviously suggesting that it be a necessary part of the educational process. Again, don't tell the Supreme Court. They seem to think that expressions of religion are forbidden in public schools.

Here's another good one. This is priceless. The Congress of the United States voted on the final version of the Bill of Rights, including the First Amendment with the "Establishment" and "Free Exercise" clauses, on September 25, 1789. ***ON THE VERY SAME DAY*** the Congress ***unanimously*** approved a resolution asking President George Washington to proclaim a National Day of Thanksgiving. That resolution reads as follows: "Friday, September 25, [1789]. Day of Thanksgiving. Resolved. That a joint committee of both Houses be directed to wait upon the President of the United States to request that he recommend to the people of the United States a day of public thanksgiving and prayer, to be observed by acknowledging, with grateful hearts, the many signal favors of Almighty God, especially by affording them an opportunity peaceably to establish a constitution of government for their safety and happiness." In other words, Congress unabashedly acknowledged the benevolence and providence of Almighty God in the founding and continued operation of this nation and directed the people of this nation to thank Him with prayer and grateful hearts. These are the very same people who – ***on that very same day*** – had just approved the First Amendment. I implore you – if anyone can see any intent by the authors of the Constitution to remove God from government, please explain it to me because I just don't see it.

Well, just because Congress asks the president to issue such a proclamation doesn't necessarily mean that he will do it. What was the response of President Washington?

First of all, keep in mind that George Washington was the President of the Constitutional Convention before he became the President of the United States. He presided over the Constitution's creation. No one would have understood the document better, nor been more familiar with its requirements, nor was more duty-bound to obey it – by virtue of both his solemn oath as president and his personal integrity. Did President Washington find any offense in this request by Congress? Well, just listen to how the proclamation which he wrote begins. "Whereas it is the duty of all Nations to acknowledge the providence of Almighty God, to obey his will, to be grateful for his benefits, and humbly to implore his protection and favor…I do recommend and assign Thursday the 26th. day of November next to be devoted by the People of these States to the service of that great and glorious Being, who is the beneficent Author of all the good that was, that is, or that will be." Separation of Church and State my – ear.

One more quick historical note on this subject. When George Washington, President of the Constitutional Convention, was sworn in as the President of the United States, he took the oath that is prescribed in the Constitution. He then added four more words to that oath which every president since has also repeated: "So help me God." He then bent over and kissed the Bible upon which his hand had rested throughout the oath. After delivering his inaugural address in the Senate

Chamber, the President and Congress proceeded to Saint Paul's Church and attended a worship service.

Volumes can and have been written to prove that the Founders never intended to remove God from government. This is a Christian nation, and the Founders never expected it to be anything else. To the contrary they knew that it **must** remain a Christian nation or it would fail. John Adams, Second President of the United States and legal expert whose work influenced the drafting of the Massachusetts Constitution and the United States Constitution, wrote, "Our Constitution was made only for a moral and religious people. It is wholly inadequate to the government of any other."

Now, on to my third point: namely, that many of the rulings of the United States Supreme Court concerning religion over the last sixty years are based upon the misguided opinions of a handful of justices and not upon a proper interpretation of the Constitution itself. Over the last six decades the principle of "separation of Church and State" has been the bedrock upon which the Supreme Court – and other lesser courts – has based its rulings regarding government and religion. Keep in mind, however, that the words "separation of Church and State" are nowhere to be found in the Constitution of the United States. It is even hard to conjure up the principle from anything written in that document. This all changed in 1947 in the case of *Everson v. Board of Education*. In that case the Court stated, "The First Amendment has erected a wall between church and state. That wall must be kept high and impregnable. We could not approve the slightest breach."

First of all, let us be careful to make a distinction between the concepts of separation of **Church** and State and separation of **religion** and State. We have already acknowledged that it was the intention of the authors of the Constitution to forbid the creation of a state church as existed in other countries. As such, technically, separation of the **institution of the Church** and the **institution of the State** is a Constitutional principle. However, we must emphatically deny and resist the notion that the Constitution intends the separation of **religion** and State. Far from it, we have already seen that the Founders most certainly intended a **marriage** between Christianity and the state. Had the Court been working to protect against the imposition of a State church, then we could applaud their stand as a bold and necessary defense of the Constitution. But this is not what has happened. In no instance during this period has the Court ruled on an attempt to create a State church. In every instance the Court has ruled on an inclusion of religion – usually Christianity – in or at some public function. This is something which the Founders and their Constitution not only permitted but encouraged; however, it is something which the Court – with a terrible regularity – has denied.

Here are a few examples of the kind of judicial rulings which have been inspired by the "separation doctrine" as conjured up by the Supreme Court . (Please note: not all of these are United States Supreme Court rulings, but they are rulings which base their findings on principles established by that Court.)

It is unconstitutional for a verbal prayer to be offered at a school even if that prayer is both voluntary and nondenominational. (*Engel v. Vitale, 1962; Abington v. Schempp, 1963; Commissioner of Education v. School Committee of Leyden, 1971.*)

The freedoms of speech and the press are guaranteed to students and teachers unless their topic is religious, in which case such speech becomes unconstitutional. (*Stein v. Oshinsky, 1965; Collins v. Chandler Unified School District, 1981; Bishop v. Aronov, 1991; Duran v. Nitsche, 1991.*)

It is unconstitutional for students to see the Ten Commandments since they might read, meditate upon, and obey them. (*Stone v. Graham, 1980; Ring v. Grand Forks Public School District, 1980; Lanner v. Wimmer 1981.*)

It is unconstitutional for a student to pray out loud over his lunch. (*Reed v. Van Hoven, 1965.*)

It is unconstitutional for a classroom library to contain books which deal with Christianity. It is unconstitutional for a teacher to be seen with a personal copy of the Bible while at school. (*Roberts v. Madigan, 1990.*)

It is unconstitutional for school officials to be publicly praised at an open community meeting if that meeting is sponsored by some religious group. (*Jane Doe v. Santa Fe Independent School District, 1995.*)

It is unconstitutional for a school graduation ceremony to include an opening or closing prayer. (*Harris v. Joint School District, 1994; Gearon v. Loudoun County*

*School Board, 1993; Lee v. Weisman, 1992; Kay v. Douglas
School District, 1986; Graham v. Central Community School
District, 1985.)*

It is unconstitutional for a kindergarten class to ask
whose birthday is celebrated by Christmas. *(Florey v.
Sioux Falls School District, 1979.)*

It is unconstitutional for a war memorial to be constructed in the shape of a cross. *(Lowe v. City of Eugene,
1969.)*

It is unconstitutional for a public cemetery to have
a planter in the shape of a cross. *(Warsaw v. Tehachapi,
1990.)*

It is unconstitutional for a nativity scene to be dis-
played on public property unless surrounded by enough
secular displays to prevent it from appearing religious.
(County of Allegheny v. ACLU, 1989.)

Sadly, the list and the absurdities go on. It all started
in 1947, and it all is based on an erroneous application of
the principle of separation of Church and State – words
that do not even exist in the Constitution. And as we
have seen, the principle has been grotesquely twisted in
such a way that it actually works against – not in favor
of – the intent of the authors of the Constitution. The
Supreme Court justice who dug deep into the personal
writings of Thomas Jefferson to unearth the phrase,
"wall of separation between Church and State" would
have been well-advised to keep digging until he also
found this wise advice given by Jefferson to Supreme
Court Justice William Johnson. "On every question of

construction, carry ourselves back to the time when the Constitution was adopted, recollect the spirit manifested in the debates, and instead of trying what meaning may be squeezed out of the text, or invented against it, conform to the probable one in which it was passed." As we have seen, the Founders intended a marriage of Christianity and State, not a divorce of the two. In the name of God and country, stop trying to squeeze some deviant and warped meaning from this honored text! The separation principle is a perversion – not a preservation – of Constitutional law, and that is not just my opinion. Consider the words and the warning of Supreme Court Chief Justice William Rhenquist in the case of *Wallace v. Jaffree*, "the greatest injury of the 'wall' notion is its mischievous diversion of judges from the actual intentions of the drafters of the Bill of Rights…. The 'wall of separation between church and State' is a metaphor based on bad history, a metaphor which has proved useless as a guide to judging. It should be frankly and explicitly abandoned."

Now, lest you think Chief Justice Rhenquist some kind of judicial kook when it comes to this subject, consider these words from Oliver Ellsworth, the third Chief Justice of the United States Supreme Court, "the primary objects of government, are peace, order, and prosperity of society…. To the promotion of these objects, … good morals are essential. Institutions for the promotion of good morals are, therefore, objects of legislative provision and support: and among these … religious institutions are eminently useful and important…. The legislature, charged with the great interests of the community, may, and **ought** to countenance, aid, and protect religious institutions … ***the legislature may aid the maintenance of [Christianity]***, whose benign influence on morals is universally acknowledged. It may be added that this principle has been long recognized, and is too intimately connected with the peace, order, and happiness of the state to be abandoned." (Emphasis added.) Imagine that! The third Chief Justice of the Supreme Court proclaimed that it was not only constitutionally appropriate but morally necessary for the State to not only protect but to aid and encourage religion. This sentiment was echoed by Joseph Story.

Joseph Story was one of the legal luminaries of the young United States. Included among his credits are these: he was the youngest Justice ever to be appointed to the Supreme Court, and served in that capacity for thirty-four years; he founded the Harvard Law School and authored many classic legal texts including his *Commentaries on the Constitution of the United States*. In that text he wrote the following about the First Amendment: "We are not to attribute this prohibition of a national religious establishment to an indifference to religion in general, and especially to Christianity, which none could hold in more reverence than the framers of the Constitution…. Indeed, the right of a society or government to [participate] in matters of religion will hardly be contested by any persons who believe that piety, religion, and morality are intimately connected with the well being of the state and indispensable to the administration of civil justice.... It is, indeed, difficult to conceive how any civilized society can well exist without them. And, at all events, it is impossible for those who believe in the truth of Christianity as a Divine revelation to doubt that it is the especial duty of government to foster and encourage it among all the citizens and subjects...." Let me repeat, it is the especial **duty** of government to foster and encourage Christianity among **all** the citizens and subjects.

I think we have made our case: (1) the Constitution of the United States is a Christian document, (2) the drafters of the Constitution never intended to remove God from government, and (3) many of the rulings of the Supreme Court concerning religion over the last sixty years are based upon the misguided and erroneous opinions of a handful of justices and not upon a proper interpretation of the Constitution itself. **That** is the truth, **that** is the whole truth, and **that** is nothing but the truth, so help us God. We **are** in the right, this **is** a Christian nation, but what **are** we going to do about it?

I have argued repeatedly throughout this short book that the glory of America cannot be revived unless the goodness of America is restored. One of the greatest obstacles to this restoration has been the conviction by many in the moral, Christian community that we are shackled by the Constitution itself – that it demands the separation of religion and the State and the divorce of God and government. Those shackles are hereby shattered. The United States and its God were always intended to be inseparable. Now that we understand this we can act upon it. That's the good news. There is bad news, however, for there is another obstacle, and this one is far graver than anything which the chains of iron or law can impose.

CHAPTER SIXTEEN

MUHLENBERG

John Peter Gabriel Muhlenberg was born on October 1, 1746, in Trappe, Pennsylvania. He received a classical education at the Academy of Philadelphia (now the University of Pennsylvania) and pursued advanced studies in Germany. Interestingly, and prophetically, he was exposed to military life when he served briefly in the German dragoons. After returning to Philadelphia he was ordained as a Lutheran pastor, but he later was ordained again into the priesthood of the Anglican Church. When the Revolution began in 1775, Muhlenberg was pastor of a church in Woodstock, Virginia. He was deeply affected by the injustice of British policies toward the Colonies and found himself drawn more and more to the cause of independence.

On the morning of January 21, 1776, the Reverend Muhlenberg stepped to the pulpit and faced his congregation. His sermon text was from the third chapter of Ecclesiastes. He read:

"To every thing there is a season, and a time to every purpose under heaven. A time to be born, and a time to die; a time to plant, and a time to pluck up that which is planted; a time to kill, and a time to heal; a time to break down, and a time to build up; a time to weep, and a time to laugh; a time to mourn, and a time to dance; a time to cast away stones, and a time to gather stones together; a time to embrace, and a time to refrain from embracing; a time to get and a time to lose; a time to keep, and a time to cast away; a time to rend, and a time to sew; a time to keep silence, and a time to speak; a time to love, and a time to hate; a time of war, and a time of peace."

At this point Muhlenberg dramatically paused. He looked sternly out at his congregation and declared, "And this is the time of war." He stepped from the pulpit, marched to the rear of the church, and removed his clerical robes revealing a colonel's uniform in General Washington's Continental Army. He announced that he would be leaving the next morning to join Washington's forces encamped on the hills overlooking the British blockade and occupation of Boston, Massachusetts. He urged anyone who felt likewise to join him. The next day he left with three hundred men who would form the core of the Eighth Virginia Regiment.

Muhlenberg's brother, Frederick Augustus, also was a minister but did not share Peter's views – until he watched the British burn down his church in front of his own eyes. Frederick experienced a change of heart that day and joined the military as well.

Peter Muhlenberg served the Patriot cause at such places as the battles of Brandywine and Germantown. He shared in the hardships of Valley Forge and fought at Monmouth and Yorktown. He ended the war as a major general.

Upon the conclusion of the war, the Muhlenberg brothers became active in politics. Peter was elected to the first United States Congress which met from 1789 to 1791. His brother was Speaker of the House for that first Congress. In January, 1801, Peter became a United States Senator.

Today, it sounds strangely foreign to read about ordained men of God serving as combatants and holding political office, but it was quite commonplace in the early years of our nation. Of the fifty-six men who signed the Declaration of Independence, over half had graduated from institutions which today would be considered seminaries or Bible colleges. Of the fifty-five who authored the Constitution, virtually all were members of Christian churches, and many were religious leaders. These were men of courage who took a stand for God and country regardless of the consequences, and for some the consequences were severe. Where have all the heroes gone?

Today, many pastors will not even address various social and political issues for fear of jeopardizing their tax-exempt status or alienating affluent members of their flock. They worship at the idol of Mammon. Others have no stomach for a fight – even righteous ones. Instead of taking a bold stand, they cower in some dark corner and hope someone else will do the fighting for them. They would be well advised to remember the judgment on the Church of Laodicea. And when the shepherds are stricken with avarice and cowardice, what hope is there for the flock? Many Christians today have grown spiritually pudgy and pusillanimous. Oh, they whine, they moan, they make sorrowful noises or express righteous indignation – and then they promptly return to the temporary comfort of their mortgaged homes and hope someone else will do the fighting for them, too. They can't get involved. There is no time. They have careers to pursue, shopping to do, soccer games to attend, and television shows that simply must be watched. Really? What will happen to your career when the nation falls? Where will you shop when the economy collapses? Are memories of a soccer championship the best future you can provide for your children? And that mindless drivel you watch – is it more important to you than saving your nation? Cowards! Fools! Our God and our country deserve better than this – but you say you have no time for them!

An interesting argument has been concocted by some Christians who apparently have no stomach for the battle that needs to be fought, and so they seek to excuse themselves with sanctimonious proclamations. They point their noses heavenward and claim to be above the dirty world of politics. Well, then, you presume for yourself a purity above that of Christ, Himself! Jesus jumped into the muck of this world with both feet. He trod the dusty trails. He hungered; He thirst; He slept on the ground; He preached from hillsides; He touched the unclean; He washed the feet of His disciples; He was mocked, beaten, spit upon, whipped, and crucified. He spared Himself none of the filth of this world. He did it for you. What was your argument, again? You want to remain above the dirt of politics? ***Shame!*** The battle of our lives is being fought on many fronts, including political ones. If we don't take the field, guess who wins!

Many Christians have lost their ardor for God. Many, but not all. As always, there remains a remnant – a faithful few who now must fight even harder, even for those who don't deserve it and won't appreciate it, because that is what Christ did for us, and now it is our turn to walk in His steps.

Our effort must be two-pronged. First, we must stand firmly for the right and unwaveringly against the wrong. We have danced with the Devil long enough, and we have paid a terrible price. Remember, the lesser of two evils is still evil. ***No more compromise!*** Compromise is simply defeat on the installment plan. We must be guided in all our public decision-making by Biblical principles and the ideals of our Founders. This is what led us to glory in the first place, and this is what will lead us back. The recommendations expressed in this book will go a long way toward accomplishing this goal. I freely confess that these recommendations are tough – even harsh at times – but our disease has progressed too far to expect easy cures. Sugar pills don't accomplish much against malignant cancers. Remember, God chastises those whom He loves.

Chastisement is never pleasant, but, if taken to heart, it will lead to reform and new life.

Second, we must answer the loving call of Christ. Whereas He never looked to governments to be compassionate (for, in truth, they cannot be – remember that coercion is not compassion), He did call on us as individuals to be compassionate. When the entitlement programs described in Chapter Four are eliminated, millions of people will find themselves in a bad way. For many it will be their own fault, and they will be able to recover quickly simply by getting a job. They are freeloaders and co-conspirators with the Deceivers and charlatans who have committed state-assisted theft. Necessity and a gnawing pain in the gut will go a long way toward reforming them and ushering them to an honorable life of responsibility and productivity. However, there will be others – especially the aged and infirm – who will not be in a position to care for themselves. This is where churches and charities **must** step into the breach. The good news is that such private organizations can handle these responsibilities much more humanely, inexpensively, and efficiently than can impersonal and corrupt government bureaucracies. The problem, of course, is that the churches and charities can only give what they get. Their effectiveness depends largely upon the generosity of the populace. The proposals of this book, once implemented, will result in several hundreds of billions of dollars being returned to the people annually. Accordingly, there will be no shortage of funds available to care admirably for the needy. Our fear lies in the stinginess of a hard heart that would deny these funds to those in need. How do we combat this stinginess? As always, Christ not only has the answer, He is the answer. If we all simply give generously, we can care humanely for the needy while enjoying an even greater degree of freedom and prosperity for ourselves. Furthermore, the nation will return to robust health and true security. Win, win, win. None of this will be possible, however, unless the Christian community mobilizes and joins the fight. There can be no conscientious objectors in a righteous war. The time has come to rise up for your God, your nation, and your families.

How do we do this?

CHAPTER SEVENTEEN

THE RUDDER: A BATTLE PLAN

John Hancock, the Revolutionary War hero who boldly set his hand to the Declaration of Independence, left this urgent plea for all generations of Americans to heed, "I conjure you, by all that is dear, by all that is honorable, by all that is sacred, not only that ye pray but that ye act."

*　　*　　*

Across the land discontent and frustration fester. Malaise is devolving into desperation. The people know something is wrong, but they do not know how to fix it. They know they must do something, but they are not sure how. The solutions presented in this book detail what needs to be done. We must stop this dangerous and destructive accumulation of power in the hands of the state and return power to the people: to individuals, to families, to churches, and to charities. We must take control of the government and commence its deliberate and systematic dismantling. We must not return the wrecking ball to storage until we have returned our national and state governments to the same dimensions they possessed in the late eighteenth century. We must then take the measures described to prevent the re-growth of this malignant weed. We must take a determined stance against crime and criminals – drug dealers in particular. We must protect our borders, enforce our immigration laws, and deal decisively with those who violate these laws. We must secure our nation, its people, and its values through a system of universal national service. We must return God to our schools and our schools to local control. We must rebuild and preserve a moral and Godly America. And we must be prepared to fight to the death all those whose ignorance or malevolence conspire to cause the death of our beloved nation. Now that we know what we need to do, how do we do it?

Many Americans look at the magnitude of the task before them and despair of ever being able to do what needs to be done. It simply seems impossible. Scarcely over one-half of the working population pays the taxes that support the other nearly one-half of the population that draws some type of benefit from the government. Have the charlatans and Deceivers secured enough dependents to insure our dark descent into socialism? It seems that we already may have passed a critical tipping point and that America the Great already may have slipped into the realm of History. To that our answer must be, ***"No! By God, No!"***

Remember that history is made by determined minorities. Some estimates claim that at the time of the Revolution, about one-third of the colonial population supported the British, about one-third supported the Patriot cause, and about one-third was indifferent. Of the one-third that supported independence, it is doubtful if more than about ten percent of them were actively involved in fighting the war or serving in some other official capacity that worked to secure freedom. This means that only about three to four percent of the colonial population (about 2.5 million in 1776) actually won the war. Keep in mind that they defeated one of the wealthiest empires on earth with the mightiest army and navy.

The rudder of a ship determines the ship's direction, but the rudder itself is a relatively small part of the ship. We don't need one hundred fifty million Americans fighting to win this war. Like the First American Revolution, we only need three or four percent of the population to seize the flag, stand boldly, and charge the enemy battlements.

The bad news is that we must confront and combat a powerful enemy that is both visible and invisible. That enemy is well-organized, well-funded, and well-connected – just like the British. By comparison we seem disorganized, impoverished, and disconnected – just like the Patriots. That's the bad news. The good news is that we already have everything we need to fight and

win the Second American Revolution. From sea to shining sea there exist thousands of bands of committed
patriots. It is a virtual army waiting to be organized and
deployed. There are TEA Parties, 9-12 groups, Christian
Patriots, American Legionnaires, Veterans of Foreign
Wars, Chambers of Commerce, Christian Businessmen
and Businesswomen Associations, along with uncounted
other patriotic and Christian groups and congregations.
They all are natural allies, and yet their provincial per-
spectives prevent them from banding together to fight
together for God and country. Leaders, seek out the leaders of like-minded organizations in your area and plan
ways to work together. Create a corps of volunteers who
are willing to serve across your organizational lines to
help elect candidates, promote worthwhile events, educate the people, support Godly and patriotic campaigns,
and protest the policies and programs of the opposition.

We must look past the few things that divide us and
focus on the noble cause that unites us. Christian and
Jew; Catholic and Protestant – all of us who pray to the
same God must now bow down to Him and rise up to
serve and defend His America. Army, Navy, Air Force,
Coast Guard, and Marine – you proudly served your
nation before. She needs you again. Patriots never get
to retire. Join a group and join the fight. Pastors and
priests, remember the proud and Godly example of Peter
Muhlenberg. Stand firm "against principalities, against
powers, against the rulers of the darkness of this age…."
Remember with fear and trepidation that you will be

judged by a higher standard. God put you here for a purpose, and that purpose extends beyond the stained glass walls of your cloister. Proclaim the Truth from your pulpits, and then, like Colonel Muhlenberg, march boldly forward to rebuild our God's America. This *is* the time of war. The opposition is formidable, but "if God is for us, who can be against us?"

Yes, *if* God is for us, who can be against us? But if God is against us, then all hope is lost. Above all we must recommit to, and devote our personal and national lives to, that Ally Who empowered us to win the First American Revolution. God must not be reduced to some inconsequential appendage to our personal belief systems. He is and must be the heart, soul, mind, and strength of our personal and national lives. He used to be. In his inaugural address of April 30, 1789, George Washington, the "Indispensable Man", proclaimed the indispensable nature of our reliance upon God. "No people can be bound to acknowledge and adore the Invisible Hand which conducts the affairs of men more than the people of the United States. Every step by which they have advanced to the character of an independent nation seems to have been distinguished by some token of providential agency…. We ought to be no less persuaded that the propitious smiles of Heaven can never be expected on a nation that disregards the eternal rules of order and right which Heaven itself has ordained…." God was the radiant core of our national life. He must be again. The Truth is that God and America the Great are inseparable. If we abandon God, we will cease to be America, and America will cease to be.

And should all this motivation prove insufficient to spur you on, look at your children. Stop reading and go, look at your children. Go to her room. Watch him play outside. Pull out a picture, or recall with your mind's eye. Remember the infant curled up in the crib. Remember the kindergartner disappearing behind the classroom door on that first day of school. Remember the sports star, the cheerleader, the graduate. Remember Christmas morning and the Easter Bunny. Remember the roller skates, the bicycles, and the family picnics. Remember the fun, the pride, the love. Remember when you were their hero. You still are. Don't let them down. What kind of life do you want for them? What kind of America will you give to them? You **must** devote time, energy, and resources to the rebuilding America the Great, and you **must** begin now! Give your children reason to thank you, not cause to curse you.

*   *   *

In September of 1814, about a week after Washington, D.C. had been sacked by the British during the War of 1812, a young attorney named Francis Scott Key witnessed what might have turned out to be the conclusive battle of that war – the British attack on Baltimore. He watched as the courageous defenders within Fort McHenry stood up against the full fury of the British fleet.

How could they possibly withstand such a savage assault? The battle raged all day and into the night. Key prayed, and he strained to see if the American flag remained over the fort. The rockets red glare and the bombs bursting in air gave proof through the night that our flag was still there. But about two hours before dawn, the firing mysteriously stopped, and Key feared the worst – that the fort had fallen. Why else would both sides have silenced their guns? By the dawn's early light he struggled to see whose colors flew over the fort. Did the Star-Spangled Banner yet wave o'er the land of the free and the home of the brave?

That question has been repeated throughout the generations, and each generation has had to answer it for themselves. Now it is our turn. Does the Star-Spangled Banner yet wave o'er the land of the free and the home of the brave? Does it? What say you, and what are you willing to do about it? As for me and my household, we will serve the Lord. As for me and my household, we will serve the United States of America for this *is* a free and Christian nation, and I intend to keep it that way. But if the United States of America is to remain the land of the free and the home of the brave, then, by God, it is time we start acting like it. So, I implore you, "I conjure you, by all that is dear, by all that is honorable, by all that is sacred, not only that ye pray, but that ye act." Stand with me, join the fight, save the Revolution, and let's give this country back to God!

Amen.

OPERATION REDEMPTION
RESOLUTION

Whereas

John Adams said, "religion and virtue are the only foundations … of republicanism and of all free governments" and "Our Constitution was made only for a moral and religious people. It is wholly inadequate to the government of any other."

Patrick Henry said, "The great pillars of all government and social life … [are] virtue, morality, and religion" and "It cannot be emphasized too clearly and too often that this nation was founded, not by religionists, but by Christians; not on religion, but on the gospel of Jesus Christ."

Charles Carroll, signer of the Declaration of Independence said, "[W]ithout morals a republic cannot subsist any length of time; they therefore who are decrying the Christian religion, whose morality is so sublime and pure ... are undermining the solid foundation of morals, the best security for the duration of free governments."

John Hancock said, "all confidence must be withheld from the means we use and reposed only on that God who rules in the armies of heaven and without whose blessings the best human councils are but foolishness and all created power vanity."

George Washington, President of the Constitutional Convention, said, "Religion and morality are the essential pillars of civil society" and "true religion affords to government its surest support" and "it would be peculiarly improper to omit, in this first official act, [Washington's first inauguration as President of the United States] my fervent supplications to that Almighty Being who rules over the universe, who presides in the councils of nations, and whose providential aids can supply every human defect .... No people can be bound to acknowledge and adore the Invisible Hand which conducts the affairs of men more than those of the United States. Every step by which they have advanced to the character of an independent nation seems to have been distinguished by some token of providential agency.... [W]e ought to be no less persuaded that the propitious smiles of Heaven can never be expected on a nation that disregards the eternal rules of order and right which Heaven itself has ordained" and "I am sure there never was a people who had more reason to acknowledge a

Divine interposition in their affairs than those of the United States; and I should be pained to believe that they have forgotten that Agency which was so often manifested during our revolution, or that they failed to consider the omnipotence of that God who is alone able to protect them" and "Of all the dispositions and habits which lead to political prosperity, religion and morality are indispensable supports. In vain would that man claim the tribute of patriotism, who should labor to subvert these great pillars of human happiness.... And let us with caution indulge the supposition that morality can be maintained without religion. Whatever may be conceded to the influence of refined education on minds ... reason and experience both forbid us to expect that national morality can prevail, in exclusion of religious principle."

Noah Webster said, "the moral principle and precepts contained in the Scriptures ought to form the basis of all our civil constitutions and laws" and "the Christian religion, in its purity, is the basis, or rather the source of all genuine freedom in government ... and I am persuaded that no civil government of a republican form can exist and be durable in which the principles of that religion have not a controlling influence" and "The education of youth should be watched with the most scrupulous attention. It is much easier to introduce and establish an effectual system ... than to correct by penal statutes the ill effects of a bad system.... The education of youth ...

lays the foundations on which both law and gospel rest for success."

Samuel Adams said, "Education … leads the youth beyond mere outside show [and] will impress their minds with a profound reverence of the Deity…. It will excite in them a just regard to Divine revelation."

Alexander Hamilton, signer of the Constitution, said, "the law … dictated by God Himself is, of course, superior in obligation to any other. It is binding over all the globe, in all countries, and at all times. No human laws are of any validity if contrary to this."

Rufus King, signer of the Constitution, said, the "law established by the Creator … extends over the whole globe, is everywhere and at all times binding upon mankind …. [This] is the law of God by which he makes his way known to man and is paramount to all human control."

Abraham Baldwin, signer of the Constitution, said, "free government … can only be happy when the public principle and opinions are properly directed … by religion and education. It should therefore be among the first objects of those who wish well to the national prosperity to encourage and support the principles of religion and morality."

Gouverneur Morris, signer of the Constitution said, "Religion is the only solid basis of good morals; therefore education should teach the precepts of religion and the duties of man towards God" and "the most important of all lessons [from the Bible] is the denunciation of ruin to every State that rejects the precepts of religion."

James McHenry, signer of the Constitution, said, "the Holy Scriptures … can alone secure to society, order and peace, and to our courts of justice and constitutions of government, purity, stability, and usefulness. In vain, without the Bible, we increase penal laws and draw entrenchments around our institutions" and "Bibles are strong entrenchments. Where they abound, men cannot pursue wicked courses."

It is clear that the Founders of this nation, including those who wrote the Constitution, believed in and intended to create an indissoluble union between the government of the United States of America and the principles of Christianity as revealed in the Holy Bible.

Whereas

On June 30, 1775, the Continental Congress passed its Articles of War which included this passage, "It is earnestly recommended to all officers and soldiers diligently to attend Divine service; and all officers and soldiers who shall behave indecently or irreverently at any place of Divine worship, shall … be brought before a court-martial."

On July 4, 1776, the Continental Congress approved a Declaration of Independence which proclaimed that "governments are instituted among men" in order "to secure these rights" which "are endowed by their Creator."

On July 4, 1776, the Continental Congress appointed a committee consisting of Benjamin Franklin, Thomas Jefferson, and John Adams to create a seal that would characterize the spirit on the newly proclaimed nation. Franklin proposed Moses lifting up his staff and dividing the Red Sea while Pharaoh and his charioteers were overwhelmed with the waters. He suggested this motto: "Rebellion to tyrants is obedience to God." Jefferson proposed the children of Israel guided through the wilderness by a pillar of cloud by day, and a pillar of fire by night.

On October 12, 1778, a Congressional resolution was passed which stated, "Whereas true religion and good morals are the only solid foundations of pubic liberty and happiness: Resolved, That it be, and it is hereby earnestly recommended to the several States to take the most effectual measures for the encouragement thereof."

On January 21, 1781, Robert Aitken asked the Congress for permission to print Bibles on his presses rather than import them from other countries. The Congress approved his request. Congress later approved the Bible which Mr. Aitken published. Inscribed in the front of that Bible was this endorsement: "Whereupon, Resolved, That the United States in Congress assembled … recommend this edition of the Bible to the inhabitants of the United States."

On August 7, 1789, President Washington signed into law the Northwest Ordinance, which had been previously enacted under the Articles of Confederation. This ordinance established the requirements of statehood for prospective new states. Article III states, "Religion, morality, and knowledge, being necessary to good government and the happiness of mankind, schools and the means of education shall forever be encouraged."

In 1789 the First Congress, which would also draft and approve the First Amendment, authorized the establishment of a chaplain for each house of Congress. These chaplains were paid with public funds and their duties included the responsibility to pray at the convening of each house of Congress. Congress also authorized the use of government buildings, including the Capitol building, to serve as houses of worship while awaiting the construction of churches in the national capital.

On September 25, 1789, Congress approved the Bill of Rights. Later that same day the following resolution was passed by Congress: "Resolved, That a joint committee of both Houses be directed to wait upon the President of the United States to request that he would recommend to the people of the United States a day of public thanksgiving and prayer, to be observed by acknowledging with grateful hearts the many signal favors of Almighty God, especially by affording them an opportunity peaceable to establish a Constitution of government for their safety and happiness…."

On October 3, 1789, President Washington – who had previously served as the president of the Constitutional Convention – issued the following Thanksgiving proclamation in response to the request from Congress, "Whereas it is the duty of all Nations to acknowledge the providence of Almighty God, to obey his will, to be grateful for his benefits, and humbly to implore his protection and favor…I do recommend and assign Thursday the 26th. day of November next to be devoted by the People of these States to the service of that great and glorious Being, who is the beneficent Author of all the good that was, that is, or that will be."

In 1853, a Report of the Senate Judiciary Committee stated, "They [the Founders] intended, by this [First] Amendment, to prohibit 'an establishment of religion' such as the English Church presented, or any thing like it. But they had no fear or jealousy of religion itself, nor did they wish to see us an irreligious people… they did not intend to spread over all the public authorities and the whole public action of the nation the dead and revolting spectacle of atheistical apathy."

In 1854, a report of the House Judiciary Committee stated, "Had the people, during the Revolution, had a suspicion of any attempt to war against Christianity, that Revolution would have been strangled in its cradle. At the time of the adoption of the Constitution and the amendments, the universal sentiment was that Christianity should be encouraged, not any one sect. Any attempt to level and discard all religion would have been viewed with universal indignation…. It must be considered as the foundation on which the whole structure rests…. In this age there can be no substitute for Christianity; that, in its general principles, is the great conservative element on which we must rely for the purity and permanence of free institutions. That was the religion of the founders of the republic, and they expected it to remain the religion of their descendents."

It is clear that the Founders and first generations of Americans, as demonstrated in the acts of the Continental Congress and the Congress of the United States, believed in and intended to create an indissoluble union between the government of the United States of America and the principles of Christianity as revealed in the Holy Bible.

Whereas

John Jay, first Chief Justice of the United States Supreme Court, said it is "the duty of all wise, free, and virtuous governments to countenance and encourage virtue and religion" and "The Bible is the best of all books, for it is the word of God and teaches us the way to be happy in this world and in the next. Continue therefore to read it and to regulate your life by its precepts."

Oliver Ellsworth, third Chief Justice of the United States Supreme Court, said, "the primary objects of government, are peace, order, and prosperity of society…. To the promotion of these objects, … good morals are essential. Institutions for the promotion of good morals are, therefore, objects of legislative provision and support: and among these … religious institutions are eminently useful and important…. The legislature, charged with the great interests of the community, may, and ought to countenance, aid, and protect religious institutions … the legislature may aid the maintenance of [Christianity], whose benign influence on morals is universally acknowledged. It may be added that this principle has been long recognized, and is too intimately connected with the peace, order, and happiness of the state to be abandoned."

William Paterson, signer of the Constitution and United States Supreme Court Justice, said, "Religion and morality … [are] necessary to good government, good order, and good laws."

James Wilson, signer of the Constitution and United States Supreme Court Justice, said, "All [laws], however, may be arranged in two different classes. 1) Divine. 2) Human. … But it should always be remembered that this law, natural or revealed, made for men or for nations, flows from the same Divine source: it is the law of God…. Human law must rest its authority ultimately upon the authority of that law which is Divine."

Joseph Story, founder of the Harvard School of Law, author of the legal classic *Commentaries on the Constitution of the United States*, and United States Supreme Court Justice said about the First Amendment, "We are not to attribute this prohibition of a national religious establishment to an indifference to religion in general, and especially to Christianity, which none could hold in more reverence than the framers of the Constitution…. Indeed, the right of a society or government to [participate] in matters of religion will hardly be contested by any persons who believe that piety, religion, and morality are intimately connected with the well being of the state and indispensable to the administration of civil justice…. It is, indeed, difficult to conceive how any civilized society can well exist without them. And, at all events, it is impossible for those who believe in the truth of Christianity as a Divine revelation to doubt that it is the especial duty of government to foster and encourage it among all the citizens and subjects…." and "Probably, at the time of the adoption of the Constitution, and of the Amendment to it now under consideration, the general, if not the univer-sal, sentiment in America was that Christianity ought to receive encouragement from the State…. An attempt to level all religions and to make it a matter of state policy to hold all in utter indifference would have created univer-sal disapprobation if not universal indignation" and "One of the beautiful boasts of our municipal jurisprudence is that Christianity is a part of the Common Law…. There never has been a period in which the Common Law did not recognize Christianity as lying at its foundations…. I verily believe Christianity necessary to the support of civil society."

It is clear that the Founders of this nation, including those who served as Justices of the United States Supreme Court, believed in and intended to create an indissoluble union between the government of the United States of America and the principles of Christianity as revealed in the Holy Bible.

Whereas

In *Vidal v. Girard's Executors* (1844) the United States Supreme Court stated,

"It is also said, and truly, that the Christian religion is a part of the common law."

In *City of Charleston v. S. A. Benjamin* (1846) the United States Supreme Court stated,

"Christianity is a part of the common law of the land, with liberty of conscience to all. It has always been so recognized.... If Christianity is a part of the common law, its disturbance is punishable at common law. The U. S. Constitution allows it as a part of the common law... Christianity is part and parcel of the common law.... Christianity has reference to the principles of right and wrong ... it is the foundation of those morals and manners upon which our society is formed; it is their basis. Remove this and they would fall....What constitutes the standard of good morals? Is it not Christianity? There certainly is none other ... the day of moral virtue in which we live would, in an instant, if that standard were abolished, lapse into the dark and murky night of Pagan immorality. In the Courts over which we preside, we daily acknowledge Christianity as the most solemn part of our administration."

In *The Church of the Holy Trinity v. United States* (1892) the United States Supreme Court stated, "This is historically true. From the discovery of this continent to the present hour, there is a single voice making this affirmation ... There is no dissonance in these declarations. There is a universal language pervading them all, having one meaning; they affirm and reaffirm that this is a religious nation. These are not individual sayings, declarations of private persons: they are organic utterances; they speak the voice of the entire people ... These and many other matters which might be noticed, add a volume of unofficial declarations to the mass of organic utterances that this is a Christian nation."

In *United States v. Macintosh* (1931) the United States Supreme Court stated, "We are a Christian people... according to one another the equal right of religious freedom and acknowledging with reverence the duty of obedience to the will of God."

In *Zorach v. Clauson* (1952) the United States Supreme Court stated, "We are a religious people whose institutions presuppose a Supreme Being.... When the State encourages religious instruction or cooperates with religious authorities by adjusting the schedule of public events to sectarian needs, if follows the best of our traditions. For it then respects the religious nature of our people and accommodates the public service to their spiritual needs. To hold that it may not would be to find in the Constitution a requirement that the government show a callous indifference to religious groups. That would be preferring those who believe in no religion over those who do believe.... [W]e find no constitutional requirement which makes it necessary for government to be hostile to religion and to throw its weight against efforts to widen the effective scope of religious influence."

In *Everson v. Board of Education* (1947), the United States Supreme Court first erected the "wall of separation between church and state" as a principle for basing its rulings; but, as we have seen from the preceding evidence, that principle is not consistent with the original intent of the Founders nor the Constitution. In *Wallace v. Jaffree* (1985) Chief Justice William Rehnquist filed this complaint: "There is simply no historical foundation for the proposition that the Framers intended to build the 'wall of separation' that was constitutionalized in *Everson*…. But the greatest injury of the 'wall' notion is its mischievous diversion of judges from the actual intentions of the drafters of the Bill of Rights…. [N]o amount of repetition of historical errors in judicial opinions can make the errors true. The 'wall of separation between church and State' is a metaphor based on bad history…. It should be frankly and explicitly abandoned…. Our perception has been clouded not by the Constitution but by the mists of an unnecessary metaphor."

It is clear that until recently the United States Supreme Court consistently upheld the belief that the Founders and the Constitution intended to create an indissoluble union between the government of the United States of America and the principles of Christianity as revealed in the Holy Bible.

Therefore be it resolved that this school district intends to honor the heritage of the United States and the legal intent of the Founders and the Constitution by enacting these ordinances to apply throughout this school district:

(1) Voluntary, non-denominational prayer shall be allowed at all school functions and at all school facilities, and

(2) Images of the Ten Commandments and the text of the Ten Commandments shall be allowed at all school functions and at all school facilities, and

(3) The moral lessons expressed in the Ten Commandments shall be taught in each elementary school class and in every language and civics class in grades six through twelve.

MORE SOLUTIONS

SPREAD THE WORD

Be a modern-day Paul Revere.

In 1775, Paul Revere sounded the alarm and spread the word to protect his countrymen against the tyranny of the British Monarchy. Today, you can spread the word to protect your countrymen against the tyranny of Big Government.

Help rebuild America the Great!

Take advantage of our bulk rates and give copies of **Solutions** to friends, family, neighbors, school teachers, pastors, libraries, and your elected officials. Distribute them through your churches, Chambers of Commerce, and other organizations.

EDUCATE AND LEGISLATE. Give a copy to your elected officials. Tell them you will not vote for them unless they publicly proclaim that they will be guided in all their official decision making by Biblical principles and the ideals of the Founders.

Call (909) 913-7878 to get a quote for volume discounts and shipping costs.

MEET THE AUTHOR

Invite Lawrence Paul Hebron to talk with your organization about healing our nation and rebuilding America the Great. Call (909) 913-7878 for details.

AND FOR STILL MORE SOLUTIONS

See our website: www.solutionsthebook.com

11245671R00116

Made in the USA
Charleston, SC
10 February 2012